WORCESTERSHIRE

1 *(overleaf)* *Worcester Cathedral, West front*

J. S. LEATHERBARROW

WORCESTERSHIRE

B. T. Batsford Ltd

London

for
Arthur and Marjorie Trippass
who brought us to Worcestershire

First published 1974

© J. S. Leatherbarrow 1974

ISBN 0 7134 2786 8

Text printed and bound in Great Britain by Richard Clay (The
Chaucer Press) Ltd, Bungay, Suffolk. Plates printed by Fletcher
& Son Ltd, Norwich for the publishers B. T. Batsford Ltd,
4 Fitzhardinge Street, London W.1

CONTENTS

	List of Illustrations	8
	Acknowledgements	9
	Map of Worcestershire	10–11
	Introduction	13
One	Worcester—the Hub	43
Two	North-West along the Teme	63
Three	South-West to Malvern and Beyond	83
Four	South-East towards the Cotswolds	108
Five	East and North-East towards Warwickshire	136
Six	North with the Severn	159
Seven	Towards the Northern Border	178
	Epilogue	202
	Index	207

LIST OF ILLUSTRATIONS

1. Worcester Cathedral, West front — *frontispiece*
2. The Cathedral crypt — *page* 17
3. Prince Arthur's Chantry — 17
4. The Guildhall, Worcester — 18
5. Berkeley Almshouses, Worcester — 37
6. Paradise Row, Worcester — 37
7. St Swithun's Church, Worcester — 38
8. The Greyfriars, Worcester — 55
9. West across the Teme — 56
10. The Malvern Hills — 56
11. Broadwas — 73
12. Martley Church — 73
13. Great Witley — 74
14. Malvern Priory — 91
15. Little Malvern Court — 91
16. Ripple Church — 92
17. Croome D'Abitot — 109
18. Pershore Abbey — 110
19. Bredon — 127
20. Broadway — 127
21. Evesham — 128
22. Evesham Abbey — 128
23. Abbot Lichfield's Campanile, Evesham — 145
24. Bretforton — 146
25. Ombersley — 146
26. Hanbury Hall — 163
27. Dodford — 164
28. Harvington Hall — 181
29. Chaddesley Corbett — 181
30. Wilden — 182
31. Glasshampton — 199
32. Bewdley — 199
33. Hagley — 200
34. Ombersley — 200

ACKNOWLEDGEMENTS

Since this kind of book is obviously dependent for its factual historical information on the writings of one's predecessors I wish, first of all, to acknowledge my debt to the late Alec Macdonald's *Worcestershire in English History*, first published in 1944, upon which I have relied heavily in the historical section of the Introduction. For historical dating and architectural detail Professor Pevsner's volume on Worcestershire in his Buildings of England series and F. J. S. Houghton's 'Little Guide', in the Methuen series revised by Mr Matley Moore in 1952, have been quite indispensable. Other substantial source books I have indicated in the text. Then there are the dozens of pamphlets and monographs written by parsons—bless them!—on their own churches. These have been of great value. For the rest, I can say that I have visited all the buildings referred to in this book. It is a sad sign of the times that I have found many of the churches locked and it is not much comfort to be told that the key may be found at the cottage of Miss Clutterbuck who may live as much as a mile away and who may be out when you call. For personal appraisements and observations as well as for small morsels of local gossip I must take my own responsibility. They will not suit everyone I know; but such judgements provide the only personal flavour to such a book and save it from being the mere catalogue which I do not believe its publishers mean it to be. I am grateful to Mr R. J. Collins for initiative and much advice and help at various stages of the book. Also to the following for their permission to reproduce photographs: Barnaby's Picture Library (Pls 5–7, 11, 13, 15, 30); *Birmingham Post and Mail* (Pls 20, 29); J. Allan Cash (frontispiece); B. G. Cox (Pl. 22); H. G. Dabbs (Pl. 12); M. Dowty (Pls 14, 28, 34); *Evesham Journal* (Pl. 21); A. F. Kersting (Pls 2, 3, 19, 26, 33); Kenneth Scowen (Pls 9, 10, 24, 25); the late Edwin Smith Pls 4, 17, 18, 23, 32); the late Miss Marjorie Wight (Pl. 31); The Worcestershire County Record Office kindly made some of the photographs available.

WORCESTERSHIRE

WARWICK

W

STAFFORD

SHROPSHIRE

Dudley

Amblecote
Wollaston
Stourbridge
Leasowes
Old Swinford
Pedmore
Halesowen
Hagley
W. Hagley
Clent
Clent Hills
Broome
Frankley
Romsley
Lickey Hills
Cofton Hackett
Wythall
Alvechurch
Bordesley
Beoley
Ipsley
Redditch
Crabbs Cross
Chadwich
Bromsgrove
Finstall
Tardebigge
Stoke Prior
Hanbury
Dodford
Grafton
Upton Warren
Wychbold
Droitwich
Chaddesley Corbett
Belbroughton
Harvington
Cookley
Churchill
Harborough Hall
Blakedown
Kidderminster
Stone
Summerfield
Wilden
Hartlebury
Waresley
Chadwick
Elmbridge
Lovett
Westwood Park
Ombersley
Hampton
Uphampton
Sytchhampton
Shrawley
Lenchford
Dunhampton
Comhampton
Crossway Green
Doverdale
Wolverley
Wribbenhall
Stour
Stourport-on-Severn
Upper Arley
Bewdley
Severn
Ribbesford
Dowles Manor
Areley Kings
Astley
Glasshampton
Great Witley
Abberley
Rock
Far Forest
Bayton
Mamble
Stockton-on-Teme
Lindridge
Stanford-on-Teme
Shelsley Beauchamp
Shelsley Walsh
Knighton-on-Teme
Eastham
Teme
Rochford
Tenbury
Hanley William
Hanley Child
Stoke Bliss

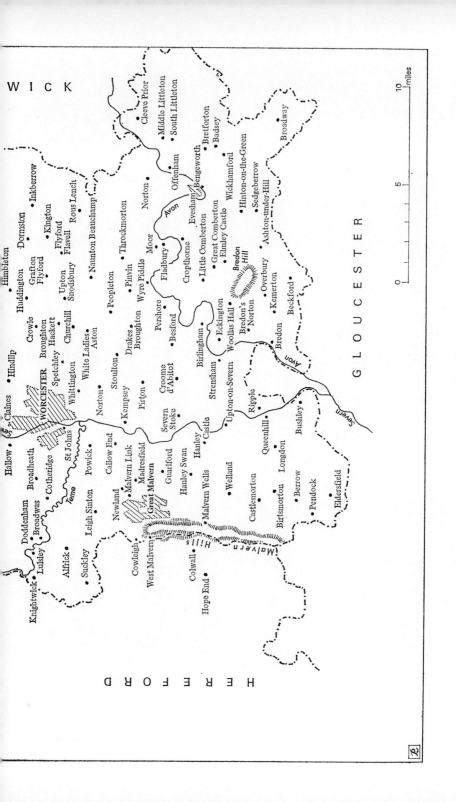

Introduction

Of the making of many county books there is no end and Worcestershire is no exception to that observation. In recent years several admirable volumes have been produced, ranging from the meticulous and massively learned guide which conducts you parish by parish through the county and unerringly points you to every building of interest; to the chatty anecdotal companion which saunters through the countryside at leisurely pace lighting up your journey with its flashes of human interest. In the constricted space available this book must necessarily fall into the second category. Why then, it may be said, add to the tally of such books in a way that is bound to produce some disappointments because of its necessary omissions?

While every age is an age of change it is just to contend that in our own that change is one of alarming rapidity and for that reason your technical guide as well as your discursive travelogue may quickly seem inaccurate. You may for example go, guide book in hand, to look for a certain mid-Victorian Gothic parsonage which the guide book notes as a particularly rich example of that exotic genre. But instead you will find a small housing estate of glossy modern dwellings complete with two garages and sauna baths. Besides, Worcestershire and every town and village locality has trenchant plans for its own reconstruction and in a few years the shape of things everywhere will be radically altered. How much poorer would the social historian be if he had no Defoe or Celia Fiennes or Arthur Young or Viscount Torrington to show him what England was like in their day. So there is a place, we believe, for books which maybe of even added interest in the future when people ask what the English counties looked like in the mid-1970s.

Worcestershire has been fortunate in its chroniclers of the past. When Habington was forced because of his complicity in the Gunpowder Plot to remain for his life within the confines of his county he considered himself fortunate to escape with his life; we consider ourselves fortunate that he devoted the rest of that life to a careful recording of the antiquities of his County. Habington's writings remain the *fons et origo* of all subsequent historians of Worcestershire. The Prattinton collection at the Society of Antiquarians' library is another rich vein of Worcestershire lore and then of course, in the late eighteenth century comes the grandiose and magisterial Nash, the classic historian of the County. Posterity has reason to be grateful for his temperate habits, for, he says, 'I was the better enabled to go through with it, as I lived within my income, and by inclination as well as profession, was restrained from elections, gaming, horse racing, fox hunting and such other pleasures as are too frequently the ruin of country gentlemen.' Fortunate are you if you possess his two handsome calfbound volumes for they are now a highly priced collector's piece much sought after for their antiquarian interest rather than for the value of the information they contain. For of course, Nash is long superseded and we pass on to those indispensable volumes of monumental scholarship, the Victoria County History, which produced its first volume in 1901 for the County of Worcester. Yet here again you may be disappointed or misled for the world has changed much since the beginning of the century and buildings which the V.C.H. describes have been restored or even destroyed and many have changed their use. And so on to our own excellent contemporaries.

Worcestershire is a small county but it holds an important place through the whole march of English history. But more than that it is a household name to many who have never been anywhere near it. There is Worcester sauce which adds a savoury touch to world-wide meal times. There is Worcester porcelain which gives delight both to connoisseurs who can afford to collect the early and scarce pieces of the Wall and Flight dynasties and to housewives who can afford to set its beautiful modern products on their dinner tables. Worcester has a long reputation for the manufacture of gloves and today it is the headquarters of one of the largest mail order firms in the world.

Other enthusiasts know it for its high-ranking cricket team and for the fact that its county matches are played against the backdrop of some of the most beautiful scenery in England. Others think of it in connection with the music of Elgar, now enjoying a revived popularity which it never quite lost even in a period when the sentiments of 'Land of Hope and Glory' were not popular.

Others will visit it in search of beautiful things, whether they be of scenic grandeur or in the art and artifice of craftsmen, ancient and modern. But the visitor must not be disappointed if he does not find the object of his search either on the grandiose or extensive scale. There are higher hills than the Malverns in other English counties and we are not plentiful in impressive churches or stately great houses.

When you have looked at Worcester Cathedral, at Pershore Abbey, sadly truncated, and at Malvern Priory shorn of its conventual buildings but marvellously retaining much of its glorious medieval furnishings in glass and woodwork and tiles, you have about finished with the great churches. Our stately homes are few and far between. Only a few adhere to the purpose for which they were built and there is still a Cobham at Hagley, a Beauchamp at Madresfield, a Sandys at Ombersley, a Lechmere at Severn End and a Berkeley at Spetchley. Other great houses like Croome Court and Hewell Grange are serving various wider social functions and others like Chateau Impney having become hotels and restaurants add their quota to the 'goodness-gracious' living of the opulent late twentieth century.

It is rather in the middling things that we excel; in a wide range of half-timbered houses such as becomes a countryside once thickly covered by timber. In middling houses, larger farms and smaller manor houses where the waxing and waning of agricultural prosperity can be traced in the building exploits of their owners from generation to generation. In middling people, neither too rich nor too poor, who work hard on their farms from dawn to dusk and yet have sufficient time and energy to support a Three Counties Agricultural Show with its own permanent ground at Malvern or its Three Choirs Musical Festival which visits the Cathedral every three years.

There was a time when Worcestershire earned a certain *kudos* as an important dramatic centre and when some of George Bernard Shaw's plays had their first production by Sir Barry Jackson at the Malvern Festival Theatre.

We must look as we travel on at a few great buildings both civic and ecclesiastical which come from more recent times. The Shirehall and Guildhall in Worcester will arrest our attention for a little while, Stourport-on-Severn contributes a fine new Council House, Civic buildings and a new Technical College complex flanking Deansway in Worcester provide a striking contrast between the neo-Georgian and the mid-twentieth century idiom. Then, of course, there is a certain amount of Victoriana, but we are not so rich in neo-Gothic churches as some counties. Stourport-on-Severn has an ambitious unfinished church by Gilbert Scott, Worcester's St. George's by Aston Webb has been much praised as has also his Malvern College library which dates from 1924.

But again, having looked at the three great monastic churches of the diocese it will be the middling churches which will sustain our interest. Of these there is a surprising profusion, some not always wisely restored, and heavily Victorianised, but nevertheless impressive, ranging from an astonishingly large crop of well preserved Norman buildings like Rock and Astley and Holt and a little cluster in the Teme valley and the south-west of the county, through a few average Georgian churches, in Worcester especially, to the superb baroque of Great Witley.

But before we go looking for details we must try and supply the whole pattern of Worcester history against which to set them, for the buildings are generally a reflection of the social organisation of the period from which they spring. To condense the whole history of Worcestershire into a few pages is an invidious task, yet obviously it is something which must be attempted if we are to understand why the county achieved its present configuration.

When the Malvern and Lickey Hills, pre-Cambrian and of the oldest and hardest rock on earth protruded from a primeval sea, Worcestershire had made its first appearance. When the sea shrank to shallow lagoons and over millions of years forests appeared and decayed the county had been furnished with the coal measures of Dudley and the Wyre Forest. Vast lakes dried out to leave the salt

16

2 (*opposite above*) *The Cathedral crypt – Norman strength*
3 (*below*) *The Cathedral – Prince Arthur's Chantry – late Gothic flowering*

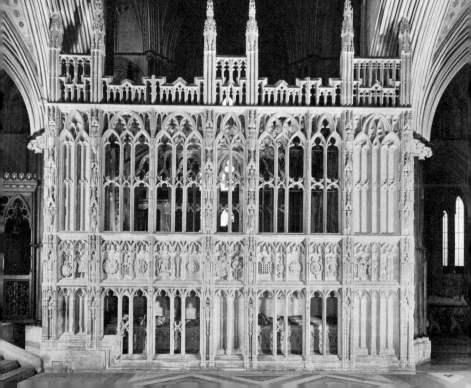

deposits of Droitwich and Bromsgrove. Sand and mud formed the red sandstone of Kidderminster and Bromsgrove and the red marl which gives the Worcester fields so much of their characteristic colouring. Later submergence gave us the deposits of blue limestone, the clays of the Avon valley and the yellow oolite of Bredon Hill. In the Ice Age, boulders from the mountains of Scotland were swept down into this countryside and when, after the Ice Age, the Severn was bent southward to the Bristol Channel, Worcestershire had assumed much the shape which we see today. But we must envisage it as covered with dense forests which survived until comparatively modern times.

The bones of prehistoric animals, marooned when the English Channel formed to separate us from the Continent, may be seen in the Worcester Museum. From Palaeolithic man of whom there are scarce traces, flint axes were found at Henwick and St. John's, near Worcester. Neolithic, Bronze and Iron Age men invaded from the Continent. Neolithic implements smooth and round have been found on the Malvern, Lickey and Bredon Hills. For the most part their owners were herdsmen and dwellers on the hills but their implements have been found in the river valleys near Bewdley and Lindridge and Broadway. The Bronze Age people, tall and fair, left their weapons along the Severn and cinerary urns have been found at Badsey and Evesham and Charlton, near Cropthorne. The Britons or Celts of the Iron Age about 600 B.C. had a simple culture of their own and their pottery and necklaces, ornaments and armlets have been found in the County. These people had their forts on Midsummer Hill, on Woodbury and Berrow, commanding the passes into the Teme Valley and one of their camps has been excavated on Bredon Hill. Burial mounds are rare; there are five on the Clent Hills and Whittington Tump near where the M5 motorway skirts Worcester would surely repay further investigation.

Roman influence in the County is probably first felt with Ostorius' Second Legion towards the end of the first century. This so-called 'Augusta' Legion with its headquarters at Caerleon probably had troops at Worcester and a stone with an inscription referring to Constantine the Great, 308–337, the first emperor to tolerate Christianity, was found near Kempsey. The great battle referred to

4 (opposite) The Guildhall, Worcester – Loyalist Baroque

by Tacitus when Ostorius defeated Caractacus may have taken place, from its description, as well on the Herefordshire Beacon as the Black Mountains, but coins dating between A.D. 286 and 311 have been found on the Worcestershire site.

When the Roman frontier moved westward into Wales, a Romano-British civilization no doubt developed behind it. There would be intermarriage and integration but the county had no substantial towns nor shared greatly in the Roman road system. Much of the county was still forest, the river valleys undrained and the population scarce.

Worcester itself at this period was a small town or village on rising ground above a ford over the Severn. There is little to suggest, in spite of the 'cester', which can be misleading, that it was substantially a place of Roman settlement. More important was Droitwich with its salt springs where remains suggest that a Romano-British merchant may have had a villa. When, in the 5th century the Roman legions were withdrawn the walled towns survived whilst the villas were destroyed. Worcester must have suffered severely.

The Jutes and Saxons invaded from the Continent and the Britons were driven over the Severn by 613. The Severn Valley settlers were part of the West Saxon tribe, the Hwicce, whose territory was roughly contiguous with the medieval diocese of Worcester. Though pagan remains are scanty, burial sites have been excavated at Upton Snodsbury, Hampton, near Evesham, Bredon's Norton on the slopes of the hill and Blockley. The Hwicce formed a vassal kingdom under the heathen Penda of Mercia but when St. Augustine reached the Severn in the 7th century to confer with the British bishops, he released a controversy which has raged ever since. Where was Augustine's oak, about which Bede wrote? Old Storridge, Rock and the Mitre Oak near Hartlebury have been claimants for the honour; but the truth is unlikely ever to be known. In 680 Theodore gave the Hwicce their own diocese with its centre at Worcester which had a certain importance because of its British and Roman traditions, though it was only an enlarged village. The first bishops were Celtic monks from St. Hilda's Abbey at Whitby and they established their first cathedral of wood and this was a centre for the training of missionaries. The monks and seculars first lived together and later became differentiated. At Worcester the monks' new church was dedicated in honour of St. Mary. The site of St. Peter's is unknown. Other smaller monastic communities were established in the 8th century at Fladbury, Bredon, Kempsey and Ripple, all being colonies of monks and seculars living together and dependent on the mother church at Worcester. It is from this period that we must mark the emergence of what became later the great abbeys of Pershore and Evesham and to these early monastic missionaries we owe the evangelisation of the county and the establishment of so many of the parish churches we know today most of which have lost all but the tiniest fragments of their Saxon origins. There are bits of Saxon carvings at Cropthorne, Rous Lench, Tenbury and Wyre Piddle and a few doubtful fragments round the Cathedral.

Alfred united the south west of England, including Worcestershire, under his rule, and resisted the next great wave of invasion under the people we call the Danes. The mythical 'every Worcester schoolboy' knows how the Danish pirates rifled the Cathedral and stole the sanctus bell and how the citizens of Worcester flayed the robber and fastened his skin to the Cathedral door. Ethelred and Ethelflaeda fortified Worcester as a protected enclosure at the request of the Bishop Wirfrith.

In the monastic revival of the 10th century St. Dunstan was made bishop in 957 but reigned only for two or three years. His successor, St. Oswald, was a much more influential figure bringing all the monastic houses including the Cathedral under the rule of St. Benedict. He enlarged the church of St. Mary and made it the seat of the Bishop. From this period begins the vast wealth of the monastery which became the greatest landowner in the county. Agriculture flourished and Worcestershire began to build up its great reputation as a land flowing richly with the produce of orchards and cornfields and vineyards. Robert of Gloucester in the time of Henry III, 1216–1272, knew something about us then:

> *In the County of Canterbury most fish is,*
> *And most chaise of wild beasts about Salisbury, I wis:*
> *At London ships most, and wine at Winchester:*
> *At Hartford sheep and ox, and fruits at Worcester.*

The county now assumed the civil configuration which persisted till the Reformation. Mercia was divided into 'shires' taking their names from administrative centres at Worcester, Gloucester, Stafford and Hereford. The Malvern Hills formed a good boundary between Worcestershire and Herefordshire but the rivers were ignored as frontiers and the irregular outline of Worcestershire with its outlying 'islands' of territory was due to the efforts of landowners, especially monasteries, to keep their lands in the same county.

When the Norman conquest came, Worcester was dominated by one of the most important figures in its history, St. Wulfstan, a monk of Worcester, who was consecrated Bishop in 1062 and as a strong supporter of William, assisted at his coronation on Christmas Day 1066; his loyalty secured him in his bishopric when Lanfranc was replacing Saxons with Normans, and to him we owe the rebuilding of the Cathedral, reluctant as he was to destroy the Saxon church of St. Oswald. The new church, with choir, transepts, crypt, aisled nave and two west towers, was consecrated in 1088. The proportions were much the same as those of the present Cathedral and Wulfstan's glorious crypt is still there for us to see today. He died in 1095, was canonised in 1203 and his tomb became associated with the usual legendary and extravagant paraphernalia of the later Middle Ages. St. Oswald and St. Wulfstan are the two paramount ecclesiastical figures of Worcester.

A word should be said about Domesday Book, for this very competent schedule for assessing the King's revenue is the best picture we have of the social structure of England at that time of the developing manorial system. Worcester was divided into 12 Hundreds of civil administration which were reduced to five by the thirteenth century. The King was the richest landowner, then the Abbey of Westminster which had profited largely by the grants of Edward the Confessor. 759 of the total 1200 hides of land in the county were in church hands and the Bishop of Worcester was the fourth richest prelate of the time. There were 15 lay landowners, mostly Normans, who lived elsewhere and one manor only was still in Saxon hands, the manor of Chaddesley Corbett which was held by a woman, Eadgifu.

Only six parish churches were mentioned in the Worcester survey, Astley, Doverdale, Broughton Hackett, Feckenham, Halesowen and

Martley, which was wrongly located in Herefordshire. This is of course no real indication of the number of churches since 60 priests are mentioned in 57 places and this is probably much nearer the right number. They were mostly to be found in the south of the county where the church lands lay; the population in the centre and north was thinner.

The eleventh and twelfth centuries were a most prolific period of church building in Worcestershire and we shall find extensive Norman remains in no less than about 30 parishes in the course of our perambulation.

We need not delay ourselves by becoming too involved in the tangled skeins of late medieval history. For Worcestershire the two names that stand out here are King John and Simon de Montfort. First however, we may note that in 1138 when Stephen attacked Dudley Castle, held for the Empress Matilda, he found it strongly fortified and impregnable. The attack failed and he contented himself with laying waste the surrounding country. In 1140 rumours of an attack by the Empress on Worcester made the citizens take refuge in the Cathedral and the chronicler Florence of Worcester gives a vivid picture of the defensive situation. Earl Waleran savagely burnt the city. In 1150 Worcester was again burnt by Stephen. Henry II restored the royal authority along the Severn in defiance of the Marcher lords, Hereford and de Mortimer. Henry was twice crowned at Worcester and at the Easter Mass in 1158 he and his queen laid their crowns on the altar. The first royal Council was held at Worcester. William de Tracy, one of the four knights who murdered Beckett, was a Worcestershire landowner.

King John was a frequent and affectionate visitor to Worcester and Walter de Grey, Bishop of Worcester and formerly the King's Chancellor, was among the signatories to Magna Carta. The leading men of Worcester declared for the invading French Dauphin in 1216 and when Ranulph, Earl of Chester, attacked the city for the king the monks were heavily fined for their support of the rebels and melted down the ornaments of the shrine of St. Wulfstan to discharge the fine. John died at Newark and expressed a wish to be buried in the Cathedral at Worcester which he loved. So there stands his tomb in the chancel of the rebuilt Cathedral, just about where the apse ended in the original church. It is one of the most notable tourist attractions in the county. The tomb case, in fact, dates from only about the time of the Reformation, but the Purbeck marble recumbent effigy, though not quite contemporary is the earliest of all royal effigies in England. The tomb was opened in 1797 and various relics were found. The remains of the King were enshrouded in a monk's cowl which the wearer had hoped might be a passport to heaven. The figures flanking the head represent St. Oswald and St. Wulfstan whose prayers, no doubt the king hoped, might assist his progress through Purgatory if the monk's cowl failed to do the trick.

In 1218 Henry III attended the rededication of the Cathedral Choir which had been destroyed in 1202. St. Wulfstan's body was placed in a new shrine which now became a principal place of pilgrimage and the increasing financial affluence with pilgrims' gifts made possible the complete rebuilding of the Norman Choir and the addition of the present Lady Chapel at the east. Here we find a superb example of the Early English style and a very early use of Purbeck marble shafts.

The Friars came to Worcester in the early thirteenth century. The presence of the Franciscans or Greyfriars who arrived in 1225 is recorded in the existing Greyfriars building in Friar Street, an exquisite restoration which should make it one of the principal objects of pilgrimage to the city. The Dominicans or Blackfriars also had their house which has entirely disappeared, though the recent excavations of Mr. Philip Barker and his indefatigable band of helpers have done much to delineate it and to enlighten us. A house of Augustine friars was founded at Droitwich in 1331. These friary houses owed much to the patronage of the Beauchamp family.

Layamon's *'Brut'* derives from this period of the mingling of the strains which emerged to constitute the developed English people, but we will defer consideration of him until we meet him on his own territory at Areley Kings.

So we come to the Barons' War and to our encounter with the other great figure of this period in the Worcester saga, Simon de Montfort. Walter de Cantelupe, the Bishop, led the baronial opposition to the king in the county and in 1263 Worcester was taken by the baronial forces. In 1264, when a new parliament was summoned with two citizens from each borough to sit with the nobility, historians see the origins of our later parliamentary democracy. We have no record of the Worcester representatives though doubtless they existed. The progress of the struggle is too involved to be detailed here. The attempt of Prince Edward in 1265 to capture Simon's son at Kenilworth gave Simon his chance, and slipping across the Severn at Kempsey he made the fantastic and hardly believable march from Kenilworth to Evesham in two and a half days. On August 4th Earl Simon's army gathered on Harvington Hill blocking the road to Evesham. Edward's army advanced, deceiving de Montfort's forces with a display of young Simon's banners captured at Kenilworth. Simon's forces, hopelessly surrounded, fought desperately. Simon was killed and his horribly mutilated body buried before the high altar of Evesham Abbey church. His modern memorial is to be seen in the Abbey grounds.

But the importance of it all was that the progress of Parliamentary democracy thus initiated went on. With the growth of the commercial middle class, towns developed which were based not on Roman sites but rather on Saxon encampments and their growth was encouraged by the grants of borough charters and market rights. Important towns were growing up round castles like Dudley and monasteries like Evesham and Pershore. Nine towns in Worcestershire had borough rights and the city received charters in 1189 and 1227 which were confirmed by successive kings. It was incorporated under Queen Mary and received its first mayor under James I. Magistrates came in Edward III's reign and parliamentary structures slowly developed, with the election of Knights of the Shire. To the Model Parliament of 1295 which was the real foundation of our modern Parliament came 16 members from Worcestershire, two knights of the shire and two burgesses from seven civil centres in the county.

The proximity of Wales, with its hordes of dispossessed Celts continually raiding across the border and continually being pressed back, is an important feature in the life of medieval Worcestershire. Up to the time of Edward I there was the increasing power of the Lords Marcher, the Clares and de Mortimers who defended England against the Welsh attacks. Worcester was the headquarters of Edward in his campaign against Llewelyn the Great in 1277. Again there was an outbreak of the Welsh war in 1282 and when Edward came to Worcestershire to prepare his expedition he stayed at Hartlebury Castle with Bishop Giffard. Llewelyn was killed in a skirmish near Builth. A further rebellion, easily suppressed, took place in 1294 when Edward held the last recorded royal council at Worcester. The King gave thanks at the shrines of St. Oswald and St. Wulfstan and made rich gifts to the Cathedral.

With the conquest of Wales and its subjugation, of which the great Welsh castles are the continuing evidence, the rule of the Lords Marcher came to an end. Welsh border raids continued to be severe and the surviving smaller castles and sites along the Severn, like the well preserved one at Holt are a reminder of the English defence against these plunder raids. With the establishment in Edward IVs reign of a Council of the Marches of Wales with its seat at Ludlow the danger from Wales gradually receded.

During the Hundred Years War the county supplied its quota of men and money for the campaigns. Sir John Beauchamp of Holt is perhaps the most outstanding Worcester figure of this period.

As the Middle Ages drew to their close the Black Death, that fearful plague which swept over England, ravaged the population of Worcestershire as everywhere else. In this county 44·5% of the beneficed clergy died. Whole villages disappeared and are now only beginning to be rediscovered through the enthusiasm of archaeologists. The plague stopped work on the rebuilding of Worcester Cathedral, as we shall discover later. But still there was 'the fair field full of folk' which William Langland saw in his vision on 'Malverne hulles' which was the north-west slope of the Herefordshire Beacon. Langland was probably educated in the monastic school of either Great or Little Malvern Priory.

The stirrings of events which produced the Reformation were felt in Worcestershire. The Lollardism of John Wycliff was rife in the diocese and Badby, a tailor of Evesham, was tried in the Cathedral for the heresy of denying transubstantiation and was burned at Smithfield.

The revolt of Owen Glendower was yet another uprising from across the Welsh border. Joined by the Frenchman John de Hangest the expedition marched on Worcester and did some damage there. But Henry IV proceeded against the rebels who had entrenched themselves in the old British fort on Woodbury Hill overlooking the Teme. When reinforcements failed to arrive they retreated across the river in confusion and many were drowned in the Teme.

The Wars of the Roses hardly touched Worcestershire. If the local aristocracy had any preference it was probably towards the Yorkist side with men like Richard Beauchamp, Earl of Warwick, who was born at Salwarpe Court, and Hugh Mortimer, a scion of the great Mortimer Marcher lords of Wigmore Castle who was lord of the manor of Kyle and Martley in the middle of the fifteenth century. It was he who probably built the fine Perpendicular tower of Martley Church about 1450 and then died fighting on the Yorkist side in the battle of Wakefield in 1459. His alabaster effigy, clad in the armour of the period and adorned with the Yorkist collar, is to be seen on the south side of the sanctuary of the church. The charming female figure in the mural painting over his head is probably his wife, who may have given some of the paintings and re-endowed the chantry chapel in the chancel for his benefit.

Robert Morton, Bishop of Worcester and Lady Stanley helped to convince the Duke of Buckingham, the supposed friend of Richard III, of the superior claim of Henry of Richmond to the throne of England and the ambitious Buckingham decided to encourage the marriage of his cousin Henry to Elizabeth of York. To advance his claim, Buckingham tried to seize Bewdley and Worcester and reached Woodbury Hill where the fords over the Teme were held for Richard by Sir Humphrey Stafford of Grafton Manor near Bromsgrove: Buckingham deserted his forces, fled and was taken prisoner and executed.

At Bosworth Field in 1485, among Richard's supporters, was Sir Reginald Bray, native of St. John's, Worcester who was knighted on the battlefield and later became Lord Treasurer. He was connected with the building of St. George's Chapel, Windsor and Henry VII's Chapel at Westminster. Also on the winning side was Sir John Savage of Elmley; did he put the crown on Henry's head or was it Stanley, Earl of Derby, whom history or legend seems rather to favour? We shall find a monument in Bromsgrove Church to Sir

Humphrey Stafford who tried to raise a rebellion against Henry and whose forfeited estates passed to Sir Gilbert Talbot.

The greatest lawyer of the day, Sir Thomas Littleton of Frankley, deserves a comment. His *Old Tenures* with the later commentary by Sir Thomas Coke became the standard book on the English Law of Property—'Coke upon Littleton'. He died in 1461 and is buried in the south aisle of Worcester Cathedral.

With the Reformation we move into the making of modern England, and in Worcester we have a very precious monument to one of the influential factors in that upheaval of English religion. In 1499 Arthur Prince of Wales was married by proxy at Tickenhill Palace, Bewdley, to Princess Katherine of Aragon. Later the pair lived together at these Marcher strongholds of Tickenhill and Ludlow until 1502 when Arthur died. We have graphic accounts of the splendours of the procession to Worcester and the funeral service there and we possess the chantry in which he is buried on the south side of the sanctuary, splendid still in spite of its being shorn of many of its ornaments and statues. It is the last great work of Gothic carving in England. It has frequently been pointed out that the history of England might have been somewhat different if Arthur had suc-ceeded his father as king and if Henry, as was intended, had become Archbishop of Canterbury. But a reformation of religion in some shape or form would doubtless have come all the same.

Katherine married her husband's brother Prince Henry by papal dispensation and Henry's agent in the negotiations was the Italian John de Giglis, Bishop of Worcester, who probably never set foot in Worcester. Wolsey, another protagonist of the period, had in early life been secretary to Sir Richard Nanfan at Birtsmorton Court, one of the most splendid historic moated houses still to survive in the county.

When Latimer became Bishop of Worcester in 1535 it was probably a welcome change from the foreign ecclesiastics who had occupied the see for short periods before him. So the destructive phase of the Reformation got under way. The great figure of Our Lady was removed from the Cathedral and despatched to London and the shrines of St. Oswald and St. Wulfstan were destroyed and the saints' bones buried near the high altar.

We reach the period of the Dissolution of the Monasteries and after the first act of suppression of the smaller houses in 1536 only the three priories of Worcester, Great Malvern, and Halesowen and the Abbeys of Evesham and Pershore remained. The county also possessed three hospitals, St. Mary's Droitwich and the Commandery and St. Oswald's in Worcester. In spite of protests from influential people that some of the monastic resources should be spared for educational and charitable purposes, by 1540 most of the buildings had been destroyed and the revenues alienated. We shall meet evidence of this destruction on our journey.

But the county was fortunate that three great churches survived. At Worcester most of the monastic buildings remain because of Henry's reconstitution of the bishopric and we have the priceless possession of Great Malvern and Pershore because the townspeople were able to buy the monastic churches for parish churches. Some of the medieval chantry schools, as at Martley, were refounded and continued to perform a useful educational function in later ages. The monks were well provided for and the Bishop as well as the Dean and the Chapter managed to hold on to most of their lands.

Of the great county families who secured a good share of monastic spoil we may mention the Windsors, later Earls of Plymouth, who were enriched by the rapine of Bordesley Abbey, the Dudleys of Dudley and the Lyttletons of Halesowen. These families, who rose to importance and wealth on monastic plunder, were to play a prominent part in the subsequent history of the County.

The destruction which was associated with the Reformation sadly proceeded in Worcester. Bishop Heath presided over the burning of Mass books, music and other irreplaceable medieval manuscripts on 23 April 1549. One priceless book had a lucky escape. The 'Worcester Antiphonar', a volume of thirteenth century music happily survived and some of its contents are still presented in the Cathedral from time-to-time. The musical tradition was amply sustained there in post-Reformation times and the celebrated Thomas Tomkins, buried at Martin Hussingtree, not far from Worcester, presided over the music from 1596 to the time of the Civil War.

Bishop Latimer, and Bishop Hooper who was also connected with the see suffered martyrdom during the Marian reaction and when

Elizabeth succeeded to the throne the Catholic Bishop Pate was deprived. Edwin Sandys, a firm Protestant, took his place and began that close connection of the family with the county which happily continues to the present time. The Queen visited Worcester in 1575 and was welcomed by Bishop Bullingham. She worshipped in the Cathedral and lodged in the Old Palace. We have a great many details about her visit which are too long to relate here, but it is worth recording for our gratification that she liked us very much and because of 'the good liking that her Majestie had of this citie, of the people and the place' she stayed rather longer than she had at first intended to do.

But what Elizabeth did not like was the persistence of the old faith in the county and the report that Worcestershire was 'much warped towards Popery'. There were many recusant families amongst the most prominent folk in the county; there was harbouring of priests and the secret performance of mass to keep the faith alive. Harvington Hall can still display the most fascinating hiding holes; Hindlip, which also had a clever apparatus for concealment, unfortunately has been demolished and rebuilt. These county families contributed members to the various Catholic plots to undermine the regime and possibly endanger the Queen's life. After the Babington Conspiracy in 1586, Thomas Habington was spared whilst his brother Edward was executed. There was persistent recusancy, which has been thoroughly studied and recorded for us in the invaluable *Transactions* of the County Archaeological Society by Mr. Michael Hodgetts, who is an expert in these matters. But nevertheless over this disturbed period of religious change it seems that there was no great change in the personnel of the clergy and the new regime on the whole was quietly accepted.

We come now to the Powder Plot in James I's early years and here Worcestershire men played a very prominent part. Catesby, a cousin of Robert and Thomas Wyntour of Huddington Court, a fine timbered mansion which still survives, was the principal instigator of the Plot. Fawkes, whose name it sometimes bears, was a stranger, a Yorkshireman, imported to implement the action. The Plot, which very likely had been carefully watched by the government from its inception, was betrayed, probably by Mrs. Habington, in a warning message to her brother, Lord Mounteagle. The chase of the conspirators through the county from Warwick, through Alcester to Huddington Court, the home of the Wyntours, described by a recent writer as 'the most picturesque house in Worcestershire', is an exciting saga of seventeenth century national history. The fugitives and the pursuers followed through Hanbury, Hewell Grange, Lickey End and Hagley to Stourbridge. Some of the conspirators then deserted and the end of the chase came at Holbeach Hall where the remaining members of the band were arrested. Eight surviving conspirators were condemned on 27 January 1606 and we may pass over the horrors that were perpetrated on them in the name of the English justice of that period.

Fr. Garnett was hidden at Hindlip Hall by Habington, who was not involved in the Plot; after a long and painful concealment, starvation eventually forced the priest to give himself up and he also suffered the cruel fate usual for Catholic conspirators. Other Worcester Catholics implicated as being on the fringe of the Plot were hanged at Red Hill, Worcester. Habington, as we have already noticed, was reprieved on condition that he never set foot outside the County again. The Jesuit Father Edward Oldcorne who was among the condemned was later beatified and a school named after him was opened in 1963.

The Puritans, at the other end of the ecclesiastical spectrum, must also be noted. They do not seem to have included any members of the great county families in their ranks, which were made up mostly of villagers and small tradesmen. There were the usual controversies about Sabbath observance, which reflected on the local scene the severe differences which were let loose all over the country by James I's liberal policy in his *Book of Sports*, and the Quarter Sessions records reveal many convictions of the sterner brethren. The Puritan Vicar of Eldersfield preached fiercely against the King's 'Indulgence'.

When Laud visited Worcester in 1634 he found much that needed reform if the Anglican system was to be strengthened. The Puritan 'lecturers' often appointed by civic bodies to supply some vital religious instruction in parishes of idle or even dissolute clergy were wielding a powerful influence which could be dangerous to the church establishment. Richard Baxter of Kidderminster is the outstanding and most honoured name in this connection and his classic *Saints' Everlasting Rest* was written at Rous Lench Court. In 1646 during the commotion of the Civil War he was pressed to take the living of Kidderminster, but, generously, would not turn out Dance, the unsatisfactory vicar there. Thomas Hall, the vicar of King's Norton, ejected in 1662 and a zealous Puritan, has among his tracts one with the intriguing title *The Loathsomeness of Long Hair* which might seem to have a certain appositeness to our contemporary situation.

George Fox visited Evesham and Worcester in 1655 and most of the independent sects were represented in the County. In their earlier stages we see the genesis of the Parliamentary party mustering for the struggle of the Civil War. Edward Winslow of Droitwich was one of the *Mayflower* party and became Governor of New Plymouth or Massachusetts and we find his memorial in St. Peter's Church at Droitwich.

It is hard to do justice to the story of the Civil War in Worcestershire, for the County played a considerable part in the progress of national events. The whole story is adequately told in Willis-Bund's *The Civil War in Worcestershire* and other books and excellent details of the siege of Worcester are to be found in the *Diary of Henry Townsend, 1640–1663* published by the Worcester Historical Society. By 1645 the use of the Prayer Book had been abolished, a Presbytery had been established and Bishop Prideaux had been deposed and was existing in penury at Bredon as the price of his loyalty and service to the King. But it was now that Worcester earned its proud title as 'the Faithful City' which it has cherished ever since and to which it bears testimony, rather unkindly, by its effigy of Cromwell nailed by his ears above the entrance to the city Guildhall. A visitor will not wish to miss that curious reminiscence.

The three phases of the Civil War are, roughly, the Battle of Powick Bridge which, in truth seems to have been little more than a fierce cavalry skirmish and the site of which we shall notice when we explore the Teme; the siege of the city and, most important, the battle which the leader of the Parliamentarians chose to regard as 'the Crowning Mercy of Worcester'.

At Powick Bridge little was achieved; more astute generalship and

the capture of the royal treasure might have been successful in bringing the war to an end as early as 1642. As for the attacks on Worcester,
it is important to remember that the city was a centre of Royalist
supply. In 1642 the Parliamentary general Waller marched on
Worcester, Colonel Sandys defied his challenge in a parley and the
trumpeter was shot dead. Waller was repulsed at Friar Gate and, the
Royalists attacking him from St. Martin's Gate, he retreated to
Gloucester.

In May 1644 the King was in Worcester staying with Bishop
Prideaux and raising £1,000 in subsidies. Waller again was sent to
attack the King. Charles evaded him and marched to Evesham where
he proposed arbitration. But now came news of the defeat of Prince
Rupert by the Scots at Marston Moor and it was clear that Charles's
fortunes were on the decline. With the capture of Evesham by Massey
in 1645 the vital line of Royalist supply from Worcester to Oxford
was cut; a few Worcestershire towns held out, but the cause was lost
and Charles entrusted himself to the Scots. Parliament called for the
surrender of all remaining strongholds, but Col. Washington, the
governor at Worcester, defiantly refused to capitulate. A force under
Col. Whalley besieged the city, which continued to resist, but in June
Oxford fell and on 22 July, after two months of siege, Worcester was
forced to surrender. It had been the first city to declare for the King
and it was the last to surrender. On 23 July the Anglican liturgy was
suspended in the Cathedral, General Fairfax received the surrender
and the city was preserved from violence and plunder.

The third phase of the Civil War in Worcestershire, and the most
violent, was in 1651 when Charles II arrived in Worcester on 22
August with the Scots army and was proclaimed King by the Mayor
at the Guildhall. He set up his court in Mr. Berkeley's town house in
the Cornmarket which still proudly advertises itself as 'King Charles's
House'. Curiously *au contraire*, Cromwell was quartered in Mr.
Berkeley's country house at Spetchley. On Tuesday, the 26th, there
was a rally of Royalist forces on Pitchcroft, 16,000 to resist Cromwell's
30,000. Lambert's forces crossed the Severn at Upton—there is a
favourite bit of county historical lore here about the crossing made
on a single plank which spanned the broken arches—and the Scots
were defeated and driven into the city. Cromwell ordered bridges of

boats to be constructed over the Severn and Teme at Powick and on 3 September the next attack began, Lambert and Dean moving from Upton and attacking the Royalists who were dispositioned at Powick. The Scots were driven back to the Teme but the Parliamentary forces could not force the passages of the river.

Charles watched the action from the Cathedral tower and rode out to Powick to encourage his forces, but Cromwell sent reinforcements to cross the river and the Scots fled to Worcester and were driven into the city. Charles countered with an attack at the opposite end of the city and drove the enemy as far as the junction of the Pershore road. But little was achieved. Cromwell arrived from the south side and forced the Royalists back to the city. At the Sidbury gate there was wholesale slaughter and 10,000 prisoners were taken. Together with many of the Scottish aristocracy the Duke of Hamilton fell and was carried to the old Commandery hospital, still to be seen, where he died. He was buried in the Cathedral. The King escaped. Slipping down Friar Street to his lodgings he managed to leave the city by St. Martin's Gate, near by. From thence he made his way via Hartlebury and Stourbridge to Boscobel, evading capture by hairbreadth escapes and his flight adding much to the folklore of history.

When the Restoration came it was a pity that Charles II was not a little more appreciative of the sacrifices of his 'Faithful City'. He appears never again to have visited it to express his thanks, but he made a contribution to the Restoration Fund of the Cathedral. Anglican services were revived and in its new Bishop, George Morley, the diocese received a fervent Royalist. There were few ejectments of clergy under the Act of Uniformity. Among the eminent writers of the period was John Gauden, the next bishop, the true author of *Eikon Basilike*, purporting to have been written by Charles I recording his meditations in captivity. Gauden has a memorial tablet in the Cathedral which includes a portrayal of the famous book. Samuel Butler of Strensham, the rabid Anti-Puritan, is supposed to have written his now unreadable *Hudibras* at Kempsey. Catholic recusants were still harried and Fr. John Wall, who had his headquarters at Harvington Hall, suffered as a result of the scandalous fury which arose because of the supposed plot revealed by Titus Oates. He was arrested at Rushock Court, hanged, drawn and quartered on Red Hill and earns the doubtful distinction of being the last Catholic martyr in England. Royalist families in the county who had impoverished themselves in their loyalty to the King's cause received little compensation and persecution of Dissenters continued.

Worcestershire was touched in a small way by the events of the Glorious Revolution. In 1688 the Council of Worcester promised support to William of Orange, which may have been responsible for James's visit in 1689 to encourage the Catholics whom he favoured and to overawe his opponents. He desired the Mayor and Corporation to accompany him to service in the new Roman Catholic Chapel but the Mayor declined. The King attempted to supersede the election of John Hough, a canon of the Cathedral, as President of Magdalen College, Oxford. Hough was expelled but later became Bishop of Worcester. Among the seven bishops who protested against James's Declaration of Indulgence was Bishop Lloyd of St. Asaph, later bishop of Worcester. The bishop at the time, Thomas, would probably have been among the protestors but he was too ill then to make the gesture. Then came the invitation to the Prince of Orange and the flight of James, but many loyal Anglican clergy were unwilling to disclaim their allegiance and to register an oath of loyalty to the new king. Amongst the non-jurors, Bishop Thomas would probably have declined the oath but he died before he could make his stand. The Dean, Hickes, refused and was deprived. Among the fervid adherents of the Stuarts was Thomas Morris, a minor canon of the Cathedral and vicar of Claines who was deprived and lived the remainder of his unhappy life at Upton. So profound was his sorrow at the passing of the old regime that when he died in 1748 and was buried in the Cathedral Cloister his grave, which attracts the wonderment of visitors, was inscribed with the single word 'MISERRIMUS', 'MOST MISERABLE OF MEN'. Could loyalty go further?

John Somers, son of a Worcester lawyer and a student of law under Sir Francis Winnington of Stanford Court defended the Seven Bishops at their trial with much skill. It was the start of a brilliant career. He represented Worcester in William III's Convention Parliament, became Lord High Chancellor in 1697 and was enrolled as Baron Somers of Evesham. He was one of the principal architects of the Act of Union with Scotland in 1707.

Local journalism makes its appearance at this time and *Berrow's Worcester Journal*, which dates from certainly no later than 1709, proudly justifies its claim to be the oldest newspaper in the country.

As the eighteenth century developed, Worcester streets began to assume the appearance which we now see. Tall red brick Georgian houses with stone quoins, sills and architraves rise on both sides of the main thoroughfares, their elegance only a little blemished by the modern shop structures at their feet. Georgian churches of considerable dignity begin to rise. We shall look more closely at these things when we walk around Worcester. Chief among them is Thomas White's Guildhall in the High Street, its principal entrance demonstrating the city's loyalty by its flanking statues of Charles I and Charles II; their adversary is exhibited with somewhat less dignity above their heads. The growth of trade produced a prosperous new merchant class which displaced the hegemony of the old county landowners and in spite of its cherished title the city and county settled down to a pretty loyal conformity to the Hanoverian regime. Bishop Lloyd proved to be a conscientious and hard-working bishop, administering the diocese well. John Wesley visited the county first in 1761 and later preached at Evesham, Dudley, Upton and Worcester. He was hospitably received, commented favourably on the devoutness of his hearers and saw his first chapel built in New Street in 1772.

Bishop Hurd, a personal friend of George III, was an outstanding literary figure, a friend of Pope and Warburton and other *cognoscenti* of the age. He was so much attached to Worcester that he declined the Archbishopric of Canterbury and bequeathed to the see the magnificent Hurd Library which is available to scholars and visitors at Hartlebury Castle. In 1724 the Three Choirs Festival in which Worcester is associated with Hereford and Gloucester was founded as a charity for the widows and orphans of the clergy of the three dioceses and happily continues as one of the premier musical events of the country to this day.

In 1788, the King, Queen Charlotte and the three princesses spent

5   (*opposite above*) *Berkeley Almshouses, Worcester* – *Caroline symmetry*
6   (*below*) **Paradise Row**, *Worcester* – *Georgian townscape*

a weekend at Hartlebury and arrived for a visit to Worcester on 5 August, when they stayed at the Palace. Royal portraits commemorate their visit. There was also a possibility that Worcester might have served as a place of refuge for the Royal Family in 1803 had Napoleon been successful in landing in this country. To this century we owe the great houses of Hagley and Croome Court, which we shall visit later, and the lesser but equally famous Leasowes of the poet Shenstone, near Halesowen, of which, unhappily, hardly any trace now remains. The eighteenth-century towns of Bewdley, Upton and Pershore and the baroque splendours of Great Witley will occupy us in due course.

The County was not greatly scarred by the Industrial Revolution, though Huguenot refugees founded the important glass-making industry of Stourbridge. Surface coal mining had been known since 1292 and Dud Dudley, who was responsible for some of the defences of Worcester during the Civil War, found the secret of exploiting coal for iron furnaces. Andrew Yarranton, the remains of whose industrial undertakings may be discovered by keen searchers amongst the woods of Astley, and Richard Foley of Stourbridge were among the pioneers of the Revolution in the County. The importance of the river Severn, navigable as far as Bewdley, cannot be overstressed as opening up the Midlands to the produce of the world as it entered the river's mouth at Bristol.

In the canal era a most important project was the Staffordshire and Worcestershire canal of 1771, which it was intended should join the Trent to the Severn at Bewdley. However, that town declined the honour in opprobrious terms and the canal emptied itself at the mouth of the Stour with the amazing rise of Stourport as a consequence. Here the visitor will discover the most delightful almost homogeneous Georgian town and the decayed canal basin is the happiest of hunting grounds for the industrial archaeologist. The Droitwich canal brought coal from the Severn to Droitwich, but the Worcester to Birmingham canal was not a great success. However, with the coming of railways, the canal era was to be short lived. The opening of the very first railway when Stephenson's route between Manchester and Liverpool was inaugurated touched the County with tragedy. William Huskisson, who lived at Birtsmorton Court, one of the most able and indispensable of the country's politicians, was knocked down and killed on the track, the first victim of a railway accident.

The railway system was slow to develop in Worcestershire, no doubt due to the suspicion or disinclination of the great landowners. The Birmingham to Gloucester line came no nearer to Worcester than Spetchley in 1840 and it was not until 1852 that Worcester was in direct communication with London. Over all, the Industrial Revolution laid remarkably little blemish on Worcestershire. It remained pre-eminently a rural county, rich as ever in its fruit production and its agriculture helped, in spite of the usual local hardships, by the various Enclosure Acts. During the reign of George III, between 1760 and 1820, 20% of the County was enclosed. There was indeed injustice to some of the smaller men and some local resistance as in other districts.

With the nineteenth century great movements of social reform brought prosperity and advancement and some measure of improvement in the condition of the working-class people. William Cobbett, the mouthpiece of social reform, visited the County in the course of his 'Rural Rides' in 1826. He is loud in his praise of Bredon Hill country and of Worcester and the Teme Valley, where he stayed with Sir Thomas Winnington at Stanford Park.

Life was not quite so idyllic in the towns. There were riots of Kidderminster weavers in 1828 and the miserable conditions in the glove trade have been illustrated for us in Mrs. Henry Wood's *Mildred Arkell*. There were Reform Bill riots in Worcester in 1831, when the mayor was struck on the head with a stone. But there were no desperately rotten boroughs and little rearrangement of constituencies under the schedules of the Bill. 1842 saw Anti-Corn Law and Chartist agitation. Of the five estates purchased at the instigation of Feargus O'Connor under his 'National Land Scheme' in 1847 and rented to individuals who were chosen by lot from the subscribers, two were in Worcestershire, at Redmarley d'Abitot and Dodford. But the philanthropic scheme was not a success and was wound up by Act of Parliament.

Municipal reform eventually corrected abuses connected with the ancient boroughs of Kidderminster and Droitwich, where the monopoly of power was exercised by a minority of burgesses and freemen and the reform of the Council at Worcester meant the abolition of many old ceremonies and perquisites. The climate of reform drove the Church, too, to begin to set its house in order. In 1839 came the Ecclesiastical Commission, which did something to iron out the inequalities of stipends and pluralities. The ten residentiary canons at the Cathedral were reduced to four and it was felt that as the Bishop did not really require two great houses he should live at Hartlebury Castle whilst the Dean took possession of the Palace in Worcester. Bishop Pepys was a stern evangelical who tried to stem the rising tide of Tractarianism, but Bishop Philpott, who ruled from 1861 to 1890, exercised tolerance and good sense and avoided the worst controversies of the later stages of the Oxford Movement. Due to him, no doubt, was the reputation of Worcester churchmanship as keeping the mean between the two extremes and exemplifying the virtues of a sweet 'middle of the road' Anglicanism. This excellent man is commemorated in Sir Thomas Brock's striking statue in the south transept of the Cathedral.

The restoration of the Cathedral was completed in 1874. It was begun by Perkins, the Cathedral architect, but fortunately in 1859 Sir Gilbert Scott, probably the greatest architect of the time, was brought in to complete it. £100,000 was raised by public subscription, the Earl of Dudley being particularly generous and energetic in the enterprise. The restoration may be criticised as having excessively Victorianised the building, and this is the complaint that may be made against those who carried out similar work on the many parish churches which we shall meet on our travels. But they did at any rate hand on to us usable buildings and not merely romantic fragments for the delectation of those who delight in the 'pleasure of ruins'.

So there, in a brief and inadequate sketch, is the whole story of the progress of history in Worcestershire. Having thus surveyed, however cursorily, the full pattern, we must now try and fit in the surviving pieces which illustrate our history. This will be primarily an archaeological exercise and archaeology is the association of history with *things* and it matters not in such an exercise whether the *thing* is a polished axe head or a façade by Thomas White. Both will help to illuminate Worcestershire for us.

We have had many predecessors in this task. Camden for example in his *Britannia* of 1580 highly praised our County—'To say all in one word, the air and soil are so propitious that it is inferior to none of its neighbours either for health or plenty (and in one point, for dainty cheese, surpasseth them), it produceth pears in great abundance, which though not grateful to nice palates, nor do they keep well, yet they afford a vinous juice of which is made a sort of conterfeit wine, called "Pyrry" which is very much drunk.'

There, in spite of our so-called sour pears which appear in the County Arms, is praise indeed and we have had no lack of testimonials from authorities as widely separate as Queen Elizabeth I and William Cobbett. Our county has been illustrated by several images. One writer engagingly compares it to a fruit tart, the hills being the edge of the tart with its northernmost corner burned black; a pretty image, but the burnt bit is really very small, for Worcestershire was only slightly scorched by the Industrial Revolution. For our purposes the image of a wheel is perhaps appropriate, with Worcester at the hub and spokes which we shall follow stretching out in all directions to the county boundaries. Crucial events happened along those spokes; let us see what the sites of them look like towards the end of the twentieth century.

CHAPTER ONE

Worcester—the Hub

The city of Worcester is the hub of Worcestershire and who could do justice to the 'Faithful City' in one short chapter? But an attempt must be made. And likewise, the Cathedral is the hub of the city and that is where we must begin. Our best approach is from St. John's whence we look towards the west end and see the great building poised on its hill with Severn flowing at its foot. This view across the County Cricket ground and the King's School playing fields is the only one that could be called spectacular, and although the west front is Victorian work of 1865 and not very exciting it is the best way of approaching the building. The north side can be viewed from along the High Street and the east end is hemmed in with buildings, but from the west we have the uninterrupted view of the whole.

So, descending the hill towards the river from St. John's, we leave on the left the big power station and the three blocks of high-rise flats which, though a little incongruous at this point, seem to mark the Corporation's assertion that Worcester is not entirely ignorant of the idiom of modern municipal building. We cross the bridge, built in 1771 and widened in 1931 and wonder how it could possibly be that such a large and busy city could only boast one bridge, creating the gravest traffic problems which ingenious gyratory systems have lately attempted to solve with only partial success. The argument about a second bridge has gone on for years and now continues interminably; perhaps some day we shall have a second bridge. Looking north up the river with the race course on our right, we do indeed see a bridge, but it only carries the Worcester–Hereford railway; and we see the power station discharging its effluent, which makes it all the more of a surprise to know that salmon are still caught a little to the south at the Diglis weir. To the north again we must note that in recent years the city has made enormous improvements in tidying up its river banks. If we approach in winter when the river frequently reaches a very high level it is not unusual to find that it has overflowed its banks, that the Rectifying House hotel is flooded and that swans are gliding over the water which was the road on the east bank of the river.

So we climb up the hill along Deansway and reach the Cathedral at its north-west porch. But first walk round the corner and note the remains of conventual buildings, probably the dormitory built upon vaults and subvaults with a passage below leading to the river bank, its wall marked with the levels to which the flooded river has astonishingly reached over the last hundred years. From these ruins, skilfully laid out in terraced paths and gardens, there is a wonderful view to the west, across the river and cricket fields, across Powick and Madresfield to the whole of the wide-spreading Malvern range; it is unforgettable, especially when the evening sun sinks behind it.

But back to the principal entrance at the north-west door, and candour compels us to admit that all that we see of the stone surfacing and a good deal of the fenestration too is Victorian and dates from the drastic though no doubt imperative restoration which finished in 1874. The view from west to east when we go inside displays a marvellous harmony of style which, though evolved over at least a hundred years, adhered very closely to the thirteenth-century model. The details of architectural development are so minutely and excellently given in so many fuller guides that this does not seem to be the place for attempting to reproduce them. Likewise, in the introductory chapter the main stages of the Cathedral's growth have been sketched and there is no need to repeat them. What the writer would think to be most useful would be to call attention to a few of the main features of the building which the visitor should not miss.

First, of course, is Wulfstan's crypt, all that remains of his great Cathedral building. Here is an array of columns and bays which affords one of the most dramatic spectacles of early Norman architecture in the country. The columns have plain capitals, there is enrichment on the top slab of some of them and the vaults are plain.

The whole county is unusually rich in this sort of Norman building and the example of Wulfstan's Cathedral must surely have spread into the parishes of the surrounding countryside for local emulation, even if it was not actually done by the same team of builders working both at the centre and in surrounding districts. There is Norman work also in the transepts, some of it as late as the end of the twelfth century. The chancel and the eastern Lady Chapel beyond it are priceless examples of the Early English period and the lavish use of Purbeck marble and stiff-leaf carving are particularly to be noted. There are different periods of building in the nave; the western-most piers on the north and south arcade show the transition from late Norman to Early English, the rest of the north arcade is Decorated, 1320 onwards and the south arcade is Perpendicular and later, that is to say from 1350 onwards.

The excellent guides, both books and personnel, clergymen and lay people, recruited by the Cathedral authorities will point out the salient features of the building. King John with his two protective saints is too obvious to be missed. Prince Arthur's Chantry, begun in 1504 and plentifully enriched with statuary is again one of our principal exhibits, and the enthusiastic Victorian might spare a word of praise for Scott's high altar and reredos on which obviously the restorers were determined not to be parsimonious when they spent £1,500 on it. The small square slab of stone near the west door denoting the resting place of the ashes of Earl Baldwin and the tablet in the north transept to Francis Brett Young and Jessica his wife, might easily be missed, but they are a reminder that the twentieth century has not been without its quota of eminent men in Worcester-shire. The really energetic will, of course, wish to climb the tower; those who are less so may adhere to the ground floor and amuse themselves by trying to spot monuments by Robert Adam, Roubiliac, Chantrey, Nollekens, the Stantons and others and by examining the stained glass in which Hardman, Powell, Clayton and Bell, Wailes, Whall and many of the great names of the last hundred years are represented. They may also await the descent from the tower of their nimbler brethren by trying to elucidate the subject matter of 37 misericords of 1379 now incorporated into Scott's Victorian choir stalls. But there is such an embarrassment here on floor level of archaeological material that it does not matter how long the younger ones stay on the top of the tower. If the interior has been exhausted visitors may stroll around the cloisters, looking for the Miserrimus stone, identifying graves in the garth, examining the not very good glass which fills the cloister windows and not, of course, overlooking the Chapter House. This is Norman work again, dating from about 1120 and is round with a middle column, the earliest use of this architectural device. Traces of medieval painting are still faintly seen on the walls. A tunnel-vaulted exit of about 1200 leads us out on to the south side of the Cathedral and College Green.

If by this time you wish to refresh yourself in the town and then return to explore the precincts you had better make your exit and re-entrance by the Edgar Tower, a noble gateway into the Green which was built in the early fourteenth century. A fine array of buildings encloses the Green. On the north side the houses mostly appertain to the King's School, but one is a canonical dwelling which was the scene of one of the most dramatically described funerals in English literature. From the last house on the left issued the unwieldy coffin of Maria Kilvert, the aunt of the now famous diarist, who was buried in the Cathedral garth on 2 December 1870. The details of Kilvert's visit to Worcester with his father and mother to attend this funeral, the hazardous progress of the coffin from house to Cathedral and the disappointing 'pickings' which fell to the diarist are one of the most joyous funeral passages in our literature.

But the buildings on the other side of the Green are of greater importance. Through the Edgar Gate on your right is a handsome house of 1730 with a suggestion of a Gibbs design which has been pressed into useful service as the contemporary deanery. The Old Palace in Deansway was the Dean's residence from the time when it was decided that the Bishop no longer required a town house. Victorian and twentieth-century deans lived there until, in the Second World War, it did duty for the War Agricultural Committee. In peaceful times which succeeded, it was obvious that no modern dean would wish to reinhabit so vast a house and this delightful dwelling near the Edgar Tower was very sensibly enlisted into decanal service.

Between this and the east end of the Cathedral are the remains of the Guesten Hall of the Monastery, which was built about 1320 and unfortunately demolished in 1859. The roof was a fine example of 1326 work and has been described by Mr. Charles, our expert in the County in medieval timber construction, as the most elegant example of medieval carpentry in the County. After the demolition of the Hall this splendid roof was inserted in the Hopkins church of Holy Trinity, Shrub Hill, built in 1863 and itself recently demolished. After much anxious canvassing a new home has been found for it in the Avoncroft Museum of preserved buildings, re-erected in this spirited new venture near Bromsgrove. It is a matter for intense relief and congratulation on the part of those who care for such things that this outstanding piece of medieval craftsmanship is not to be lost. But at one time it seemed a very near thing.

The next building on the south side of the Green is the large and grandiose Refectory of the Monastery now known as the College Hall and used extensively for assemblies of the King's School as well as for ecclesiastical and other gatherings. It dates from the mid-fourteenth century, has of course been heavily restored, but contains at least two noteworthy features. One is the reading pulpit on the north wall with a tiny ribbed vault and angel boss, from which the monks were read to as an aid to digestion, and the other is the magnificent life-size carving of Christ-in-Majesty which, though scandalously mutilated, retains sufficient of its lines to make its subject decipherable and which, from the stylistic evidence of its draperies, shows it to date from about 1220. In spite of its mutilation it is still one of the finest things of its sort in England and its re-use by the builders of the Monastery in the fourteenth century shows that they must have thought highly of it, too.

On the north side of the Cathedral there is an L-shaped block of Georgian houses enclosing a green and known as Cathedral Yard, in which housing has given place to use as offices. There remains however, No. 10, as a canonical residence and this is of some interest as being a Caroline house built upon the foundation of the monks' charnel house and chantry chapel which was swept away at the Reformation. Canon Davies, who has the best possible reason for knowing what is under his cellar floor, is convinced that the topmost cadavers are those of Civil War soldiers which were placed over the monastic bones after the Battle of Worcester. But this mixture of bones must rest in peace; not the most persuasive of King's School boys could induce the Canon to procure for him a memento skull from the collection.

This must now be all for the Cathedral and its precincts and we must go forward to explore as much as we have time for of the rest of Worcester. There has been a great deal of demolition opposite the north side of the Cathedral in recent years of buildings not of much value, for we hold no brief for Victorian or even Georgian slums, and it is worth examining with some care what the architects, Russell, Hodgson and Leigh, have devised for this most important sector of the city. Our own judgment is that they have been highly successful; the Giffard Hotel has been pushed as far back as was practicable, and the wing which comes away from it at right angles displays such skilful fenestration that, though it in no way imitates the true Georgian of some of the building nearby, is sufficiently sympathetic not to provide a glaring and unpleasant contrast. It must be said that the view of the north side of the Cathedral from the wide picture window of the lounge of this new hotel is a most striking *coup d'oeil* across the grass roundabout planted with trees. All this could have been so very much worse than it is and those who care for the modern configuration of the city, especially in relation to the focal point of the Cathedral, must be deeply grateful for the skill of those who have devised such a satisfactory solution to what must have been a delicate problem of townscape planning.

Our perambulation of Worcester may again be conveniently conducted under the image of a wheel, with its radial spokes starting at the Cathedral hub. The easternmost runs beneath the east end of the Cathedral, where a street of tiny Georgian houses may be noted and various antique shops inspected, to the famous Worcester Porcelain works and its admirable museum. The works welcomes visitors, who are admitted to all the processes of manufacture at times conveniently advertised, and the museum, housed in adjacent buildings, should certainly not be missed. The admirable researches of Mr. Henry Sandon, recently published, have given us a definitive study of the origin and development of this celebrated ware. The industry was founded by 15 Worcester gentlemen led by Dr. John Wall, who appears to have been a gentleman of considerable versatility. It is certainly not true that he started the water cure in Malvern, but his publications on the subject of Malvern water did something to popularise it. He was born at Powick in 1708, educated at Worcester Cathedral School and Worcester College, Oxford. He was one of the original physicians at the newly founded Worcester Infirmary. Whatever his part was in the initiation of the water cure it certainly appears that his chemical experiments at 33 Broad Street, Worcester, enabled him to evolve a formula for improving the manufacture of china so as to imitate the delicate products of the East. Upon his researches it may be said that the later immense importance and popularity of Worcester china was founded. He died at Bath in 1776 and is buried in Bath Abbey.

The next spoke, N.E.E., leads us along Sidbury and towards the site of the Sidbury Gate and the bloody battle of Worcester in 1651. The principal objective here is the Commandery at the bottom on the left. This was one of the medieval hospitals, St. Wulfstan's, founded in 1085, outside the walls. What remains is the large Great Hall, timber framed and with screens passage. There is a fine oriel window and charmingly patterned glass of the late fifteenth century. There is an Elizabethan staircase leading to an upper room with early sixteenth-century wall paintings with saints and other religious motifs. It will be remembered that the Duke of Hamilton was brought here to die after the battle.

Running off Sidbury at the top is Friar Street, the next spoke, and this leads us directly into the heart of our half-timbered Worcester. The Giffard buildings and the tall multi-storied car park on the left flaunt their challenge to the medieval, but persevere, and soon you will find yourself in a veritable little enclave of the late middle ages with black and white buildings picturesquely seated on both sides. On the right you will notice Laslett's Almshouses, a twentieth-century block which is a temporary interruption, and then comes Greyfriars, certainly one of the City's most remarkable buildings. The Franciscans came to Worcester in 1239 and had been long there when this house was procured for their use, perhaps as the Guest House of the Friary for it dates from the end of the fifteenth century. Its upper floor jetties towards the street, supported by coved brackets. There is an archway into a courtyard with a garden beyond and the projecting wings at the back are probably Elizabethan. The hall is on the ground floor, its windows overlooking Friar Street, and there are two magnificent rooms above, reached by an Elizabethan staircase.

After the Reformation the building underwent many changes of fortune. At one time the Street family, of whom sprang the distinguished Victorian architect, lived there and then, by the twentieth century it had declined into a conglomeration of shops and dilapidated apartments. Then came a singular stroke of good fortune when the property was acquired by the late Major W. J. Thompson, who gave it to the County Archaeological Society, and Mr. and Miss Matley Moore, uniquely the only brother and sister Fellows of the Society of Antiquaries, came to live there and set off on the long task of its complete restoration and rehabilitation. Today, of course, it is a masterpiece of loving antiquarian care, furnished with beautiful things which the owners have assembled there. The garden beyond the courtyard which they have devised in a comparatively small space with infinite skill is an unbelievably beautiful oasis in the heart of commercial Worcester. The beneficence of Mr. and Miss Matley Moore does not stop there. The latter has purchased and restored other timbered houses in the vicinity and let them in such a way that they shall be usefully employed whilst preserving the appropriate setting for the larger building. In 1966 these benefactors crowned their work by handing over the property to the National Trust for the perpetual enjoyment of a public who are at present allowed to view it on stated occasions. It is much to be hoped that the civic authorities will value this monumental generosity, especially by finding ways in which the ancient thoroughfare with its priceless buildings can be defended against the depredations of twentieth-century heavy traffic which it was never designed to carry.

There are other smaller timbered buildings to be noted both in Friar Street and New Street, which continues it. On the other side of Friar Street from Greyfriars and a little further towards Sidbury is a component of the City Museum, not long opened, where a collection of archaeological objects, furniture and utensils, is being built up. On the east side of New Street is Nash's House, a tall, three-storied half-timbered merchant's house of the fifteenth century. The Nash family who numbered the County's historian in their ranks were pioneers in the glove-making industry; we shall meet them later, when we see how they blossomed out into landowners at Pudford and Martley in the Teme Valley, but a practical demonstration of their good heartedness is to be seen a little further down New Street where a notice marks the entrance to Nash and Wyatt Almshouses. Opposite their former dwelling house is the Market Hall of 1849. Further along on the same side is the first Methodist chapel of 1772 now fallen on sad days and, at the bottom, past the Swan with Two Nicks (or necks) King Charles' House, where that much harassed monarch made his headquarters during the ill-starred 1651 campaign and from which he escaped, with great luck, through St. Martin's Gate, to his adventurous journeyings which finished on a fishing smack on the south coast and then exile.

Now we must return to the Cathedral and set out again along the north spoke which is the main thoroughfare of the city. It will be useful to the visitor to denote that it begins at the Cathedral as High Street, then becomes the Cross and the Foregate, then Foregate Street, the Tything and the Upper Tything. All very confusing at first, but soon comprehended and absorbed as the essential Georgian Worcester. There is the little half-timbered enclave of Fish Street which lies behind the left-hand side at the beginning of the street and the big square Georgian house on the corner whose preservation and restoration is a matter of relief. And as you turn to the left off High Street to look at these timbered buildings – the Farrier's Arms is Jacobean – you pass St. Helen's, which in spite of its medieval foundation is substantially a Victorian church with a great east window by Preedy overlooking the High Street. This church has long been redundant, but it serves as the County Record Office where the archivist, Mr. Sergeant and his assistant, Miss Henderson, dispense rich treasures of county antiquarian lore to the student, with the utmost expedition and courtesy. We cannot imagine a better use for a redundant church than as a Record Office nor such an office more efficiently managed than St. Helen's by these admirable people and their staff.

On the left-hand side of High Street is the incomparable Guildhall with its Civil War reminiscences and its great carved trophy in the pediment. How splendid it would be if we could view this as a whole across long expanses of lawn, but even in its pinched-up condition among the shops and its most distant view only from across the road it is a striking achievement by Worcester's own architect, Thomas White, who designed it in 1718. The other great building along this stretch is the essentially Caroline block of the Berkeley Hospital, founded in 1697 and built in 1703. This is a long way down, in the Foregate; although so short a time separates the Guildhall from the Hospital it is remarkable how architectural style seems to have changed in less than 20 years.

But it may be convenient now to desert our radial topography for a page or two and to deal with Georgian Worcester as a whole. We are frequently told that Worcester is a priceless half-timbered medieval city; and this is true, but we must also insist that it is still a very gracious Georgian town and the depredations of latter-day developers have by no means entirely filched it from us. Let us look at some of this graciousness. First, the churches, for Worcester has rather more than a usual share of fine classical churches. We will start with Thomas White, already mentioned in connection with the Guildhall. On the authority of Nash he was certainly deeply influenced by Sir Christopher Wren, though the connection between them is hardly likely to have been as close as Nash suggests. White excelled as a stone carver; we see his expert hand in the Guildhall and Britannia House. St. Nicholas, at the Cross, is attributed by Pevsner to Humphrey Hollins, though previous writers have attributed it to White and its west end certainly has features which correspond closely to the Guild-hall. His management of the tower with squares and octagon and curves is extremely ingenious and Pevsner thinks that he cribbed it from Gibbs. Again Pevsner would deny us All Saints, near the bridge, which we have always attributed to White and would award it to Richard Squire. We know that the 'battle of styles' was acrimonious in last century government buildings so we had better not engage in a battle of architectural historians, especially as there is little space to pursue it here even if both sides could adduce adequate evidence. Elucidation is made difficult, as Mr. Howard Colvin has warned us, by a lack of differentiation at this time between the roles of designer, builder and craftsman. Be all this as it may, All Saints is a big building, with aisles and interior colonnades and a sturdy tower recalling Wren's plainer style and a huge east end, flanked by Doric pilasters with portions of an entablature and a pediment above. Nor must we overlook, sky high though it is, the bust, surely by White, of Bishop Hough who got All Saints built.

Then there is St. Swithun's, built between 1734 and 1746 which used to be attributed to White but which again he has lost in favour of Edward and Thomas Woodward of Chipping Campden. Here truly is one of our civic treasures, as well for its architecture as its fittings. As a whole piece it is delightful; most of its fittings are original and include a monumental three-decker pulpit. After some years of rather dreary neglect it is now, once more, in good order and keeping. May Worcester long continue to treasure it! Finally there is St. Martin's built between 1768 and 1772. This was designed by Anthony Keck, the architect of the Royal Infirmary whom we also meet in the remaining bit of the eighteenth century church by the river at Upton, namely the upper stage of the tower and the cupola. This St. Martin's is very much in the Gibbs tradition, with its rusticated windows, echoing its namesake in Trafalgar Square; inside, it has been a little spoilt by Gothic alterations but it resembles St. Martin-in-the-Fields, also, in the vaulting, springing from square blocks of entablature decorated in the Ionic order.

But let us now walk around these Georgian streets and take a look at some secular buildings. We have already glanced at the much buffeted White's Guildhall, but it is unlikely that anyone will deny him Britannia House, the nucleus of our famous Alice Ottley School which together with the Boys' and Girls' Grammar Schools and the King's School have made Worcester a favoured place for Grammar School education. Now they have been joined by Secondary Schools of equal quality and the City may well be proud of its educational network. Above the Britannia House portico White certainly carved the Britannia figure which gave the house its name. Paradise Row is an attractive bit of Georgian ribbon development and, returning to the Cross, with its back to Trinity Street is the wholly delightful premier Gothic Revival house of Worcester. It cannot be later than the 1770s, with its windows Venetian but having their middle light ogee headed. Strawberry Hill cannot have it all its own way and when we penetrate into the country, particularly to Croome Church, we shall see that the Gothic Revival is, as here, showing itself in Worcestershire.

But our *crème-de-la-crème* is surely 61 Broad Street. Taking its place in a dignified Georgian street façade – or at any rate it was until later day commerce messed it about – we have a four-storied Georgian house of only one bay width whose big quoins emphasise the narrowness of the building. There is a Venetian window on every floor, and then, on top of it all, a little domed belvedere with pointed windows in three directions. This joyous confection deserves a little more research for nobody seems to know anything about its provenance. The gentleman of the lowest bust earns a metaphorical salute each time we pass for it is an irresistible reminder of those Wesley busts which are so much sought after nowadays as collector's items. It would be exciting to discover that there was some Wesleyan significance in the building of this house and it is to be hoped that our cultural watch dogs will keep a good eye on its preservation.

We trust that this Georgian digression has not greatly misled our explorers, and in truth most of it lies around that north–south axis of the city which was the spoke we were following on this part of our journey. We will follow it a little further to the north to where it becomes Foregate Street and the Tything, for we must certainly take a respectful look at the massive and severe Shire Hall of 1834 by Charles Day and Henry Rowe. We cannot miss it on the right, nor Queen Victoria in sculptured lace who stands in front on guard ('Very vulgar'—as we once heard a couple of sixth form grammar school boys say, giving her Majesty a contemptuous glance as they passed). But there really is something symbolically great about all this, for *pace* our superior sixth formers, she was a very great woman, by every dimension and it seems as though the massive Grecian building behind her typifies the massive programme of social improvement and imperial and commercial expansion which was to gather impetus in a reign which was to begin soon after the building was completed. Local government, like all other government was changing for the better in the 1830s and because Greece was the sum of all the civic virtues it seemed only right that this new symbol of local government should be Grecian. So we have the fine ashlar stone

8 (*opposite*) *The Greyfriars, Worcester – fifteenth-century timber*

and the massive portico of six fluted Ionic columns supporting the pediment. Worcestershire produced in its Shire Hall no unworthy symbol of its newly found constitutional dignity.

The Royal Grammar School, a little further along, is a conglomeration of buildings with the brick Georgian Priory House as its nucleus and Victorian Gothic and twentieth-century buildings surrounding it. All this is on the site of a Cistercian Nunnery called Whiteladies, founded by Bishop Cantelupe about 1250. St. Oswald's Hospital of 1873 is another of the six sets of almshouses which Worcester possesses.

But there remain at this end of the spoke two Worcester squares of some architectural pretension which merit our attention. St. George's Square, a cul-de-sac on the east side of the main road, leads our eye instinctively to Aston Webb's great church of St. George of 1893. This is a superb design which deserves far more specialist architectual description than we have room for here, but perhaps we may call it the finest (late) Victorian church in Worcester. The dignified brick houses, mostly semi-detached and dating from the 1830s are a splendid foil leading up to a fine architectural climax in the church.

We must cross the road, however, and explore behind the shops which line the pavement so as not to miss Britannia Square. Here is something which is entirely worthy of its London counterparts, and had the late Regency builders persevered we might have had something in Worcester to rival Bloomsbury and Mayfair. The houses date from the early 1820s and are all stuccoed. They come in all shapes and sizes, detached and semi-detached and display pilasters, Grecian key patterns and all varieties of classical detail. At one time this square wore a somewhat shabby and neglected air, but it has been rediscovered in recent years and is becoming a sought-after neighbourhood with its property fetching very high prices. One after another, in obvious new ownership, one observes evidence of restoration and redecoration revealing the good taste and appreciative care of their owners. But the rescue of such a colony is by no means plain sailing, as some of these new proprietors are finding. As one remarked recently: 'It is Queen Anne at the front and Mary Ann at the back'. Certainly stucco covers a multitude of building sins. But Britannia

9   (opposite above) West across the Teme
10   (below) The Malvern Hills – Pre-Cambrian and oldest on earth

Square is a noble building conception and steadily it improves in quality and appearance.

Returning on the same side to Foregate Street one encounters the Star Hotel which follows pretty much the same building theme. This was the premier hotel in Worcester before the episcopally named hotel at the other end of the spoke came to challenge its pre-eminence. Francis Kilvert stayed here in 1870 on the night before the famous funeral and there is a poignant description of the way in which the diarist was kept awake during the night by the piercing screams of some poor young woman on her way to a more permanent home at Powick. The exterior is stuccoed, has three and a half stories and nine bays. Inside are the elaborate cornices and fluted door cases with rosettes at the corners, and a handsome staircase rises from the hall. There is much of this neo-classical building in the County. The marble fireplaces and fluted door cases appear in many of the larger farm houses and smaller manor houses which were being enlarged and rebuilt in the more settled period which followed the Napoleonic wars and the waxing prosperity of farming.

Three new buildings in this area warrant attention before we leave it. Messrs. Kay and Co., the headquarters of a world-famous mail order business built up by Isaac Wolfson whose vast fortune has been applied to many good causes, have two large premises here. The later one, neo-Georgian, dates from 1938, the earlier from 1907 is awarded the palm by Pevsner as the best building at Worcester by far of that date. The third is the Swan Theatre, between Britannia Square and the river where local dramatic enthusiasts were successful in raising such a sum as would procure a building adequate for their purposes in a light and inexpensive modern idiom. They are much to be applauded for it.

We return to the Cathedral for our last journey along the western spoke which leads past All Saints Church to Broad Street and thus to the bridge again. An extremely interesting complex of modern buildings occupies most of this spoke, which is called Deansway, but our first call must be at the first large building on the left, now known as the Old Palace, housing a comfortable club and many diocesan offices and before that, in turn, the city residence of the Bishops of Worcester and later of its Deans. No one surely is going to deny to

Thomas White the credit of the 1730 façade here, with its segmental pediment on flat Doric angle pilasters; it is so very obviously of his style. But this is only an introduction to a remarkable building. Inside you find yourself in the thirteenth-century house of Bishop Giffard with its spacious and splendid Great Hall and undercroft. The Hall is much restored, but the carved corbel heads with their grotesque features are worth examining and the overmantel of the fireplace with its two allegorical figures infilled with patterns of pseudo-Jacobean strapwork. But the undercroft is quite unspoiled Medievalism with four bays of rib vaulting. It is a pity that it should be known as 'The Abbot's Kitchen', for Worcester never had an abbot and the undercroft of the Great Hall would be the last place to find a kitchen. From the great west window of the hall is another of the stupendous Worcestershire views, across the river and the cricket fields to the immemorial Malvern Hills.

A stroll down Deansway gives us the opportunity of taking in and comparing two points of view on modern building. On the right is the Police Headquarters and the Fire Station, neo-Georgian of 1941; the worst that could be said about it is that it is competent but unadventurous and slightly dull. But in the Technical College on the opposite side, built throughout the '60s and early '70s there is adventure enough. Jettisoning any truck with traditional styles and ornament it rises up massively in a series of great cubes built of a curious yellow-green material. To the traditionalist it would of course be anathema, perhaps an evidence of architectural ideology at the end of its tether. But Pevsner's is probably the juster estimate; 'It hurts a little,' he says, 'but one should accept it if one has faith in the validity of architecture in the 20th century.'

Among all this varied modernity there survives, a little forlornly, the Countess of Huntingdon's chapel which still presents the Preservation lobby with an unsolved problem. It dates from 1804 and is full of handsome furnishings. But has it sufficient architectural merit to be worth fighting for? And is Worcester the place for a reminiscence of that formidable 'Elect lady', described as the St. Teresa of Nonconformity who almost tamed a Hanoverian King and Queen into respectability? King George II thought that she might well have been made a bishop but as the priesthood of women was no more in favour in the mid-eighteenth century than in the General Synod of the 1970s, the matter got no further. Selina (it sounds almost impertinent to call her so) visited Worcester in 1769 and found 200 adherents of her sect. As a result of her visit, a first chapel was built in 1773. In the last century the congregation did a great deal of useful charitable work and conducted vast Sunday Schools in what was then the densely congested and poverty stricken neighbourhood of Birdport. It even subscribed £11. 3. 9 towards the Worcester Memorial to Lord Nelson.

This brings our tour of Worcester streets to an end. There is much more of interest which restriction of space compels us to omit. A few paragraphs about Victorian buildings and modern industry shall conclude the chapter. Worcester is not rich in monuments of the Gothic revival. Indeed the Y.M.C.A. building on the west side of the river built in 1868 by W. Watkins of Lincoln at a cost of £4120 is about the only substantial exercise in this genre. Not unimpressive. The curious Norman-style St. Clements, in Henwick Road, was built in 1822, a reminder that the nineteenth-century medievalists experimented very early in this style and, as in other places, dropped it quickly; it did not at all please the Ecclesiologists. St. Barnabas, Rainbow Hill is red brick of 1884 and unremarkable, but St. Martin, London Road, by Fellowes Prynne, 1903 and much like his St. Alban, Bournemouth, is a more impressive job, sturdy, lofty and rock-like with some ingenious internal planning. St. Paul, usually known as 'in the Blockhouse' is a large red and black brick building which came out of Street's office, more likely by his son A.E., than by the great George himself. It was the scene of the remarkable ministry of Studdert-Kennedy, better known as the First World War padre, 'Woodbine Willie'. This is an area of demolition and municipal reconstruction and the future of this church is much in doubt. It is to be hoped that it may be preserved for it is a handsome Victorian specimen. No doubt, however, attaches to St. Peter's, 1836, of brick with stucco dressings and its detail plain, badly proportioned and mean in every way. Already (1973) it has been closed for worship; shortly it will be demolished and there will be nothing to regret there. St. Stephen, Barbourne by Preedy in 1861 is of red sandstone, large and well placed and with Hardman glass in its east and west windows.

St. Andrew, Deansway, except for its spire, disappeared long ago, but we are glad that they left that and it looks well now, standing in a public garden and a curious foil to the great modern blocks of the Technical College which flank it. But the spire, which is 155 ft. high, is one of our Worcester treasures. The tower on which it stands is Perpendicular and has fine mouldings, but the spire by Nathaniel Wilkinson dates only from 1751. But again, we are glad that they let us keep it for it is truly a Worcester landmark; and what should we do without our 'GLOVER'S NEEDLE'? Holy Trinity, Shrub Hill, by Hopkins, 1863, has recently been demolished and it is a relief that after much doubt and fear, the superb fourteenth-century roof of the Cathedral Guesten Hall which it carried for a hundred years has found a safe resting place amongst the other preserved buildings in the Avoncroft Museum. We have not much to show in the way of modern churches in Worcester; but there is at any rate one that has replaced Holy Trinity. It is known as Holy Trinity and St. Matthew, Ronkswood and it was designed by Maurice Jones and built in 1964. It is circular with a spike on the roof; no slavish imitation of medieval or Georgian models here, but we have a marmalade pot just like it.

A few observations on Worcester industry have the final word. China manufacture has already been noticed. There was probably glove-making in the thirteenth century and the craft was incorporated in 1497. It was reorganised in the nineteenth century by John and William Dent, who established their factory in what had been the mansion of the Warmstry family. Fownes gloves began in Worcester in 1777, removed to London but came back to its native place in 1884. The work still goes on. Worcester Sauce dates from the early nineteenth century; it is supposed to derive from a recipe belonging to a nineteenth-century member of the Sandys family and later commercialised at vast profit by Messrs. Lea and Perrins. The recipe is still a very carefully guarded secret. Messrs. Heenan and Froude, Archdale, Ward, the Metal Box Company, etc. have all added a mead of commercial prosperity and a variety of industrial buildings, large and small, good and bad, to the city's architectural panorama. But industry in Worcester, as elsewhere, is in a state of flux and uncertainty at present. There is much demolition and much speculation as to new road systems about which it is impossible to write as plans alter almost daily. And above all, there is the ever recurrent and apparently insoluble problem of 'the new bridge'. But in much change and demolition it does appear that Worcester citizens have a real care for what is worthwhile and should be abiding. Whatever changes take place Worcester is certain to be always a tourist attraction. Mistakes have been made; true. Good things have been allowed to decay and disappear about which infinitely greater care should have been taken. But the Cathedral is still there and there is much of the fascinating late-medieval, half-timbered city and the gracious Georgian town. Many people will come to see Worcester for years to come.

CHAPTER TWO

North-West along the Teme

We leave Worcester and begin to follow the spokes in an anti-clock-wise direction and the first shall be the river Teme which flows from a north-westerly direction to meet the Severn near Powick Bridge; and first we must cross Worcester bridge taking the Malvern road through St. John's until it crosses the new Powick Bridge. This was built in 1837, but its fifteenth-century predecessor with its three arches of sandstone still stands near by. Here we are at the site of the first clash of arms of the Civil War in Worcestershire, the story of which has been fully told by Willis Bund. A convoy of treasure consisting of plate from the Oxford colleges arrived at Worcester on 16 September 1642. Pursuing Parliamentarians had they captured Worcester and the treasure then might have finished the war. But there was poor leadership on the part of Essex, their general, and Colonel Fiennes who obtained his permission to attack the city was easily repulsed. Fiennes then crossed the Severn and camped at Powick to keep Worcester under observation. On 22 September Prince Rupert attacked the surprised Parliamentary forces and a confused skirmish took place which probably lasted no more than a quarter of an hour. But it was a fierce skirmish, the first blood-letting of the war, and both sides claimed it as a victory. All the Cavalier officers except Rupert were wounded and 50 Parliamentary troopers were killed or drowned in the Teme. The rest retired down the Severn to Upton.

We are told that on the day before the skirmish, sightseers from Worcester walked out to Powick 'to see the soldiers', and the saintly Richard Baxter who accompanied them 'out of curiosity' improved the occasion by taking the opportunity to preach a sermon. No such attractions can await us in this first stage of our exploration of the Teme, but at any rate we may view the site of the 'battle' and look at the old bridge which was there when the encounter took place. But having seen the point at which the river enters the Severn we must now return as far as St. John's at Worcester so as to follow more closely along the eastern bank.

We have two routes at our disposal. We may take the westerly road through St. John's which is the main road to Hereford; or we may travel a little to the east along the B2404 and note some parishes of special interest on our way. On the first route we pass through St. John-in-Bedwardine, now a very large Worcester suburban parish with a church which originated in the late twelfth century. There is some Decorated and Perpendicular work, but large Victorian additions with galleries in 1841 and 1884 have made the building very much a hotch-potch. Cotheridge, the next parish along the road, has a church which is, unusual for Worcestershire, whitened outside, and a very good timbered tower of which the lowest stage may be as early as 1300. The body of the church, which is Norman, has some excellent sculptured details.

Broadwas, further along the river, is worth a longer pause. A great deal of the church dates from 1200 and is fine Early English work and the south chapel, a chantry founded in 1344, has some delightful Decorated mouldings. One of the principal glories of this church is the particularly fine and unspoilt patterns of Malvern tiles in the chancel. The Priory, as we know, did an extensive trade in these tiles in the fifteenth century and they are to be found in churches over a wide area. It is pleasing fancy to think of some wealthy parishioner paying a visit of devotion to the Priory and then stuffing his saddlebags full of tiles at the Priory shop for the adornment of his own church, just as we come away with souvenirs of black pottery from Prinknash or perfume from Caldey. Monks in every age have to live.

Further along the river on its western bank we come to Knightwick, which lost its medieval church in 1867 but which was compensated with a very run-of-the-mill neo-Gothic building now a funeral chapel in 1879. The Norman font from the previous building is still there and a communion cup and paten of 1676. The Georgian rectory survives near by and the Talbot Hotel on the east bank is a good headquarters for fishermen. When we cross the fine modern bridge which replaces an earlier one which still stands we are in Herefordshire.

If we take the alternate easterly route we cross the Worcester Bridge, follow the line of the Severn and turn left about a mile along the road at the Martley turn. The first village we reach is the modern collection of houses known as Broadheath, rapidly expanding as a convenient Worcester suburb. It would be a pity here to miss the birthplace of Sir Edward Elgar where an excellent little museum of *memorabilia* is assembled. The church of 1903 is a tidy little piece of modern work, and the weather vane on its tower which is in the unusual form of a ship is a reminder that the local landowning family of Britten who had much to do with its building were navy people. We find their home a little further along the road at Kenswick Manor. Kenswick had its own chapel, which was demolished about 1860, and the manor looks like a Jacobean gabled house with a large Victorian addition at the rear. Straddling the road at this point is the parish of Wichenford through which the Laugherne brook winds its way to join the Teme. Set amidst lush water meadows is its pretty church, heavily Victorianised and with a spire added in 1863 but retaining a few traces of its Norman and thirteenth-century origins. The unescapable feature here is the Washbourne tomb of 1632 and not very good work. It is wholly of wood and rather crudely coloured by later hands. The Washbourne family lived at the nearby court, which is a fine Caroline house now stripped of most of its furnishings which went to Kenswick Manor, the neighbouring house which the present landowning family preferred to inhabit. There is a handsome timbered dovecote here which is now the property of the National Trust.

About six miles from Worcester we meet the boundary of Martley parish and here, no less in private duty bound as in the interests of truth, we must explore this territory, bounded by the Teme on the west, which is of considerable interest. This is a wide-spreading parish with no real nucleated village, but a scatter of small hamlets extended over a large area. One of these, Kingswood, now consisting of four or five timbered houses clinging precariously to the steep slope of the river bank was once a place of much greater importance. When the Teme was fordable at this point it was the first hamlet to receive travellers who, having stopped in the village of Clifton, were on their way to Worcester. The making of a new main road crossing the new Ham Bridge a little further up the river soon reduced whatever small importance Kingswood possessed and now only the foundations of a couple of dozen or so cottages survive in the woods for those who care to search for them. Some were still occupied within the memory of aged local inhabitants.

But the parish of Martley has a fair sprinkling of those 'middling' houses which are one of the delights of the County. Shortly beyond the boundary on the Worcester road is Laugherne House; the nucleus, which was a small timbered farm, survives, hugely enlarged in the mid-eighteenth century, with a fine stone façade incorporating Doric columns and a pedimented doorway. This house now accommodates the junior part of the Royal School for Deaf Children whose seniors are at Edgbaston. Barbers, a little nearer the centre of Martley is a handsome Queen Anne house which in former times was a farm and then a genteel school for young ladies. Now it is in the fortunate ownership of a gentleman whose impeccable taste maintains both house and gardens in exquisite condition. Martley Court, nearer the centre of the village, a large farmhouse, has a prim Georgian front with pediment which conceals a much older house with a panelled room which may have been a centre for the dispensing of manorial justice in this wide-spreading parish in earlier times.

Beyond the village, perched on rising ground between the Clifton and Great Witley roads is the Noak, once the estate house of a small estate within the great manor of Witley. When the prosperous glove-making family of Nash, collaterals of the county historian, quitted Worcester city, they settled first at Pudford, a stone house of the seventeenth century built on the foundations of a grange of the nuns of Westwood who had a small estate here which passed at the Dissolution to John Pakington. The house still stands as a farm in the remote reaches of the valley near the Shelsley boundary. But in the seventeenth century the Nash family built their own house nearer the village and their descendants doubled its size with a sturdy Victorian Gothic front in the middle of the nineteenth century. This was an unfortunate enterprise, for the family found themselves unable to maintain this large establishment in modern economic conditions and the estate was broken up in 1938. The Nashes of the Noak wielded a strong influence in local affairs for a long period and are still regarded with a certain whimsical affection. Never again would there be such a one as the old squire who could ride his horse up the narrow twisting Jacobean stair.

Truth to tell, the centre of Martley is not much of a place, only a pub, a post office and a petrol station with a few small houses and modern bungalows scattered around. But a mention of the workhouse or 'Union' must not be omitted because for a century the name of Martley only suggested this sinister connotation. It arose from that revolutionary measure of the Reformed Parliament which allowed a group of parishes to unite to provide a centre for the administration of the new poor law which was one more attempt to solve the ever-recurring problem of England's poor. So there the building still stands, erected in 1838 in brick, still in a Georgian style and enshrining heaven knows how many Dickensian memories of wretched old age, insupportable poverty and unwed mothers and their children. All this came to an end in the 1940s and the deteriorating buildings did service a little longer for storage and some housing. They are due for total demolition at the present time and new dwellings will no doubt furnish opportunities for happier family lives on the site of so much misery. Undoubtedly modern Martley was a good deal shaped by the presence of the workhouse in the midst.

But the glory of Martley lies in its ancient church and rectory. The church is built of a locally quarried brilliant scarlet sandstone which, a recent writer waxing eloquent, says 'has to be seen to be believed'. This is all very well but the local stone was so extremely friable that it has presented parishioners with almost insupportable financial problems of restoration and maintenance ever since. The church obviously owes its origin to the missionary labours of the monks from Worcester who are supposed to have baptised earliest Anglo-Saxon converts in the nearby 'St. Peter's Well'. As in most of these parish churches no Saxon traces remain, but in some of the Norman work we seem to see echoes of Wulfstan's crypt in the Cathedral. The nave walls are substantially Norman of the early twelfth century, but there was evidently a great rebuilding about 1315 when the church received a new east wall and window and a superb new timbered roof which still survives. The Bishop of Worcester visited then to reconsecrate the church and its three altars. Martley church was fortunate in that it had to wait until 1909 for its restoration when Sir Charles Nicholson carried out a superb and conservative piece of work. It would have been a different story if the ecclesiologists had got at it in 1850. Everything that was put in the church was of the highest quality and certain important discoveries were made. One of the medieval altars, now restored to service, a sacring bell and an incense boat were found hidden under the floor and the best of the Malvern tiles were rearranged along the footpace. Most striking of all was the uncovering of a series of wall paintings, heraldic designs, a splendid Annunciation, a visit of the Magi, and, incorporated on the south wall of the chancel, a female figure, perhaps representing the widow of Sir Hugh Mortimer who built the splendid Perpendicular tower about 1450 and who died fighting at the Battle of Wakefield in 1459. His alabaster effigy clad in Yorkist armour lies beneath. Most important are the curtain patterns on the east wall with symbolic figures from the medieval bestiaries inserted into the loops. A modern expert says that these paintings are possibly the best examples of such work extant in this country.

The ancient rectory on the east side of the churchyard is of almost equal interest. Mr. F. W. B. Charles, the county expert on timbered buildings, assigns the nucleus of the house to the early fourteenth century, perhaps the time when the reconstruction of the church took place; but each succeeding generation seems to have set its mark on it. The great hall was divided horizontally in Elizabethan times and a splendid Elizabethan staircase was built to reach the upper rooms. A side of Sir Hugh Mortimer's tomb chest with array of armorial bearings serves as an over-mantel and there are reminiscences of the Vernons and Hastings who between them held the living and supplied rectors for the best part of three hundred years. Sir Charles Hastings, founder of the B.M.A., lived in this house as a boy. The name of the priest who first built and occupied this parsonage house in the fourteenth century is a matter of conjecture; with infinite sadness the author of this present book bows himself out as the last rector to live in the ancient rectory of Martley.

The priest of a chantry chapel created within the chancel of the church taught the first scholars in a school which was situated in the N.W. corner of the churchyard and which attained a certain eminence as a Grammar School in the seventeenth and eighteenth centuries. The school was extinguished and its building demolished with the coming of popular education and the building of a new elementary school on the main road in the 1840s. Its endowments accumulated sufficiently to build in 1913 another Chantry for educational and social purposes, and when a grandiose modern school was opened in 1962 to serve several contiguous parishes its name was further perpetuated in the Chantry County Secondary School.

The road to the east out of Martley rises steeply through the hamlets of Berrow Green, Hipplecote and Collins Green to the summit of Ankerdine, one of the highest vantage spots in the County. Here is a viewpoint of surpassing grandeur. In front lies the whole range of the Malvern Hills; on the right is the Teme Valley with Bromyard and Herefordshire beyond and on the left the flat valley of the Severn looking beyond the river to the distant Bredon Hill and the Cotswolds. The road's descent to the river and Knightsford Bridge is extremely steep—the most difficult gradient for motorists to negotiate in Worcestershire. A little past the summit there is an abandoned sanatorium, a reminder that the conquest of tuberculosis is one of the most striking medical advances of our time. At the foot of the hill is what is generally known as Knightwick church, an 1856 building by A. E. Perkins which replaced the demolished church of Doddenham. There is risk of confusion here for the true Knightwick Church is the one across the river at which we have already looked and which serves mainly for a funerary chapel for the graveyard which surrounds it.

Having now met the Hereford road again we may as well cross the river and look at three Teme-side parishes on its western bank. Here we are in a heart of the hop-growing country. When Nash described Martley in 1781 he said, 'the Rectory is one of the most valuable in the county, especially in a good year of hops when the profits may amount to a thousand pounds'. He would have been surprised to know that now there is not a single hop grown in the parish of Martley. But they are here, not far away, at Suckley and Alfrick and Leigh Sinton. Hop-picking used to be a time of some trepidation to the villagers when crowds of folk, whole families, descended upon them from the Black Country, 'making a holiday of it', to pick the hops. They were times when tempers could be exacerbated and a local farmer's barn went up in flames on one occasion after a dispute with hop pickers on rates of pay. That was in the recent past, but hop pickers for the most part are now no more. Hops are picked by machinery and not by hand; the first ingenious machine for the purpose was made here at Suckley, at the Brough.

Hopyards (not 'fields', as in Kent and elsewhere) may be contracting in Worcestershire, but the growing of cider fruit is on the increase. Bulmers, the celebrated cider makers of Hereford, have bought up many acres in this neighbourhood and planted thousands of apple trees for their purpose.

Suckley church is something of a surprise. The old church was demolished in 1878 and a grand new building by Hopkins in the late geometrical style took its place. It would grace any Birmingham suburb. There is good stained glass by Kempe in the chancel and the communion cup and paten date, like so much Worcestershire plate, from 1571, which must have been a bonanza year for the silversmiths.

Its daughter church of Alfrick, for long separate as a parish but now joined up again, retains a charming little medieval building, with a little Norman work and also Decorated and Perpendicular windows. There is a north transept and vestry by Aston Webb in 1895 and the windows in recent restoration have been inserted with many panels of Flemish glass of the sixteenth and seventeenth centuries. Exemplary restoration of this small church has made its interior as beautiful as may be found in the County.

Alfrick itself has its daughter church at Lulsley, where a not very distinguished church of 1892 replaced an earlier building. Regrettably, as the prevailing habit is, this has now been declared redundant.

Leigh Sinton possesses an extremely good Norman church full of beautiful things. There is later Decorated work including the tower, but the glory of the church lies in its monuments and especially the Christ figure, recently restored. It dates, according to Pevsner, who disputes the earlier date of 1100 with the Victoria County History, from about 1220 and he declares it to be a re-set coffin lid, the head of the effigy missing, the arms a little out of alignment but the drapery in good order. There are good recumbent effigies with kneeling figures. The frontiers of Leigh Sinton bring us to the outskirts of Malvern, but it will be more convenient now to retrace our steps back over the Knightsford Bridge and Ankerdine Hill to Martley.

To the west of the centre of the village of Martley the road diverges. If we follow the left hand fork and cross the Ham Bridge we are led through some spectacular river scenery to the village of Clifton. Well named is this place, perched on a high and steep cliff above the Teme valley. It was a place of some importance in the middle ages for Henry III granted it a borough charter, a weekly market and a yearly fair in 1270, but it failed to grow. It remains a village of considerable charm, unlike Martley, a nucleated village with a substantial street and green. The old manor house of the place is embedded somewhere in the present Red Lion Inn and the church is substantially of the thirteenth century with a later shingled spire. The cross-legged knight is probably Ralph Wysham of Woodmanton in the parish. His house can still show a former chapel, timber framed and with a wagon vault roof. The church also boasts a tablet by Grinling Gibbons to Henry Jefferys of the nearby Ham Castle, now a farm rebuilt in the present century; but the tablet is not an outstanding example of his work.

We must visit the Shelsleys and therefore make our way back towards Ham Bridge and turn to the left, passing the modern farm which retains the name of Ham Castle, a previous building on the site, before reaching the bridge which takes us over the river to Shelsley Beauchamp. This red sandstone church is mostly a rebuilding by Cranston in 1846, but the tower belongs to the fourteenth century. For its early date it is a surprisingly good bit of Victorian Gothic and the discovery of a stone altar inserted at that time is something of a surprise. But on the opposite side of the river, if we can believe that Shelsley Walsh has any other claim to fame than that of the site of a popular motor cycle hill climb, there is a veritable medieval gem waiting to be visited. This is a tiny church, built of tufa with a Norman nave and a thirteenth-century chancel. But it is the chancel and parclose screens which are the main delight. Of one composition, the top rails are beautifully carved with a running vine pattern and the original rood beam above the screen is similarly highly ornamented. This little, out-of-the-way church thus contains some of the finest pre-Reformation carving in the county. Obscure and hidden away as it is, Shelsley Walsh Church should not be missed.

From Shelsley Beauchamp a steep road running east towards the high ground on the other side of the valley takes us past extensive and somewhat regrettable if necessary quarrying to a high point on the Martley Hillside road. Turning left we travel towards Great Witley; a backward glance gives us another spectacular view of the Malverns. At night this view has its own particular attraction when the myriad lights of Malvern are seen strung across the hillsides like giant sparkling necklaces.

Now we approach one of the most baleful and fascinating places in the County. The story of Great Witley is a long one and we must linger here for a longer time. When Richard Foley in the guise of a travelling fiddler appropriated the secrets of the Swedish iron industry and returned with them to Stourbridge, he was able to plant industry in the County and build up one of the first of the great Worcester fortunes of modern times. It has been wryly pointed out in defence of those who believe that history repeats itself that the last owner and inhabitant of the great house, Sir Herbert Smith, had in his youth, likewise played the fiddle in the orchestra of the Kidderminster Theatre. However that may be Richard's son Thomas bought the Great Witley estate from the Cookeseys in 1655, another Thomas rebuilt a Jacobean brick house in 1683, was created Lord Foley in 1712 and died in 1732.

The eleventh Lord Ward and first Earl of Dudley bought the estate in 1835 and made a palace out of the house between 1859 and 1861. Samuel Dawkes was responsible for the grandiose Italianate building. W. H. Nesfield laid out the gardens and terraces and James and William Forsyth, Worcester sculptors, created the mammoth fountains.

In these surroundings the Dudleys provided a setting of incredible magnificence and luxury for Victorian royalty and aristocracy.

72

11 (*opposite above*) *Broadwas – Decorated South chantry chapel*
12 (*below*) *Martley Church – Norman nave: Perpendicular tower*

Many surviving older people on this countryside worked in the house and gardens in the days of their splendour and these reminiscences of the old people are fascinating. Many a cottage boasts a photograph of some shooting party at the Court where Edward Prince of Wales occupies the middle of the front row surrounded by trophies of the *battue* and serried ranks of the Dudleys and their guests. With bated breath the old ones can still talk of the 'goings on' at the Court and of fabulous parties where the guests were each supplied with a gift from Cartiers, while the miners and ironworkers of the north of the county and the Black Country laboured to supply the wherewithal. The Edwardian period was one of great extremes of poverty and wealth and nowhere was it better exemplified than in the saga of Great Witley. But 1914 was soon to be knocking at the door and in the economic egalitarianism of the later twentieth century what remains of Witley Court is a fire-scorched and weather-beaten ruin.

An aged and rheumy countryman under the encouragement of one or two pints at the Crown could be induced with no great difficulty to relate one of the lascivious experiences of his youth. He would tell how after delivering a wagon-load of straw at Witley Court he was led by the steward along corridors and back stairs— ('Would ee loike to see a soight?'—'Now oi didn't know what sort of a soight oi were going to see') to some vantage point on the roof, where he beheld the young sprigs of Edwardian nobility splashing in the basin of Forsyth's fountain in a state of complete and carefree nudity.

But ruin awaited this bastion of a premature permissive society. A story current in the neighbourhood, probably apocryphal but none the less nice, speaks of Sir Herbert Smith, the Kidderminster blanket tycoon, dining at the Court with the Earl of Dudley—'Ye know, me lord,' he is reputed to have said, 'I could buy you up.' 'Then why don't you?' was the prompt reply. Whereupon the tycoon's cheque book was produced and Sir Herbert Smith became, there and then, the owner of Witley Court and grounds which he appears to have maintained in decent state until 1937, when disaster struck. In the absence of the owner fire broke out in one wing and destroyed part of the building. In the event it is probable that subsequent theft and vandalism did more damage to the building than the fire. Since then

13 (*opposite*) *Great Witley – Baroque splendour*

it has stood a gaunt and obscene ruin. But one thing survived almost miraculously, for it was connected to the ruined house, and that was the parish church. So Great Witley retains what has not unjustly been called 'the finest baroque church in Britain'.

When 'Timon's Villa', as Pope called it, the palace of the princely Duke of Chandos, completed in 1722, was demolished in 1747—an astonishingly short life of 25 years—it was fortunate for us that Lord Foley, an intimate of Chandos, bought some of the fittings for his newly built Chapel at Witley. Some of the iron work went to St. John's, Hampstead; the hexagonal pulpit, the lectern and some of the panelling went to Fawley in Buckinghamshire, where the local squire built a new chancel to receive them and where they may still be seen. But from the palace of Cannons at Little Stanmore near Edgware some of the choicest bits came to Worcestershire. The chapel windows, bearing the signature of J. PRICE, 1719, designed by Francisco under the influence of Ricci and Laguerre, are among the treasures. Three large and 20 small paintings in the ceiling are by Antonio Bellucci and the wonder of the thing is how all the piece-meal bits were so perfectly fitted together, perhaps by the architect Gibbs. The pre-Rococo panels are white and gold and what seems to be stucco on the ceiling is in fact *papier maché*, a recent Birmingham invention which made it possible for Bagutti to copy the Cannons stucco and allow for modifications and adaptations. So now we can only stand and marvel.

Victorian furnishings such as benches, lectern and pulpit are by Dawkes, who refashioned the Court, and the marble font, as also the fountains in the grounds, are by James Forsyth. A reminiscence of Handel, who was the Master of Music at Cannons, is the case of the organ upon which he played. The three silver sanctuary lamps were a thank-offering of Lady Dudley for the safe return of her husband from the South African war. Over all this improbable baroque splendour, so surprisingly to be found in the midst of a quiet Worcestershire countryside, presides the grandiose monument to Lord Foley by Rysbrack. With superb self-confidence as the creator of so much magnificence, and who would grudge it him, he reclines proudly and magisterially as he surveys it all. The day is long past when medieval or Elizabethan grandees lay placidly on their tomb chests and catafalques, shall we say enjoying their well-earned rest or awaiting in humblest of postures the decisions of the final judgment. Lord Foley is far too self assured for that; in life he was monarch of all he surveyed. Why should he not oversee it in death?

From the lugubrious ruins and the glorious church we retrace our steps along the treacherous road to the Stourport Lodge gates. But there is hope yet for this sad place. After years of canvassing the ultimate fate of Witley Court it seems that a stabilising operation may be carried out so that the buildings become a 'controlled ruin'. The approach drive is likely to be properly re-surfaced, the Court area to become a picnic playground and the hundreds of visitors who come annually to feed upon the delights of English baroque which the church offers are sure to be greatly increased.

But we must return to the Teme and our exploration along this spoke leads us past the Georgian Hundred House Hotel, where in former days local justice used to be dispensed, which has now transferred itself to a handsome purpose-built Court near by. Ascending the hill road, which is surrounded by scenery almost Alpine in character, we pass the entrance gates of Abberley Hall, which is now a rather grand preparatory school for boys. The Italianate mansion built by Dawkes about 1846 was the home of an opulent Lancashire cotton magnate Joseph Jones who had bought it from the Moilliets, a Genevan banking family. Joseph was succeeded by his cousin John Joseph, who added the west wing and the porch and in 1883 built the exceedingly high clock tower, so that, it is locally said, the *nouveau* cotton spinner could overlook the demesne of the rather less *parvenu* Earl of Dudley.

Abberley has two churches, the modern one of 1850, rebuilt by J. J. Cole after a fire in 1876, the older one with its nave ruinous but its chancel well restored and roofed for occasional services. There is some Norman work here and the chancel dates from the thirteenth century. It was in a crevice in the ruined walls of the nave that, a few years ago, a workman chanced upon an interesting and lucrative discovery. There came to light five silver spoons of fourteenth-century craftsmanship. Exciting indeed, but who was to profit from this astonishing find? A coroner's jury sat in solemn state in the Hundred House Court and heard the evidence of a local antiquary and an

77

expert from the Victoria and Albert Museum. Their judgment was that the spoons were 'treasure trove' and devolved upon the crown. The finder was handsomely rewarded and a facsimile set of spoons was presented to the Bishop of Worcester. But how came those spoons to be hidden in the wall? It is a fascinating speculation for some storyteller. Were they a bit of plunder, hidden in emergency by some thief in the troubled campaign of Owen Glendower, to be reclaimed in quieter times? Then was the thief himself killed in the battle and thus unable to recover them? Or was a careful rector safeguarding his household treasures in violent years? Imagination may play freely round the subject but the truth will never be known.

Abberley also possesses one of the very few pre-Reformation rectories of the county, still inhabited by the incumbent. The hall roof appears to be of the early sixteenth century, there are traces of the original solar wing and of the original kitchen which stood a little apart from the rest of the house. A piece of painted glass in the solar displays the name of John Blamyre who was rector from 1514 to 1545 and probably responsible for alterations to the house. A splendid restoration of this ancient house a few years ago made it more comfortable by modern standards and provided a dwelling place of unique traditional interest for the twentieth-century priest.

The Elms, on the right side of the road as we proceed to Stockton, is a large Georgian house which in recent years has achieved a very high place among provincial hotels with the reputation of providing some of the best cuisine outside London. At Stockton where we meet the Teme there is a Norman nave, a fourteenth-century timber porch, a brick chancel of 1718, a very good Norman south doorway and some small Norman panels near the chancel arch. Among several good monuments the strangest is the rather odd tomb of Thomas Walsh, made entirely of wood, which has its counterpart at Shelsley Walsh.

Stanford-on-Teme near by is one of the few 'Strawberry Hill Gothick' churches of the county, built by James Rose in 1768; not a bad specimen of its kind. We are in the Winnington territory here, a family who represented the county in Parliament and exercised much influence hereabout. The family home, Stanford Court, was rebuilt after a fire in 1886, but is now devoted entirely to commercial uses.

Among the remaining churches whose parishes flank the river between here and Tenbury there is an astonishing amount of fine Norman detail. At Knighton we find the characteristic flat buttresses and the south doorway has a four bay arcading above; the windows also display interesting detailed Norman work and at the west end is a sturdy wooden screen which adds support for the bell turret. A churchyard cross with a niche for receiving the Blessed Sacrament in outdoor processional ceremonies should be noted.

At Rochford, Norman work again predominates and the feature here is a tympanum with flat carving of the Tree of Life. To be noted also for connoisseurs in a very different idiom is the handsome eighteenth century mahogany organ case. At Eastham the Norman church is built of tufa and the carved panels of Sagittarius and Agnus Dei and two other motifs are an unusual find. It would be interesting if more could be discovered about these churches of the Teme Valley. From Martley onwards to the north they are notable pieces of Norman work showing close affinities with one another. Is it possible that there was a strong and well-organised band of masons trained by and working under the monks at Worcester and despatched along the river valley to replace Anglo-Saxon structures with something more up to date and more worthy of a revivified faith which stemmed from Wulfstan's rebuilding at Worcester?

Lindridge has a rebuilt church of 1861; its handsome Georgian parsonage, alienated now from ecclesiastical use, has assumed a fresh traditional distinction by calling itself a Priory. Bayton and Mamble, though somewhat further east from the Teme, may be mentioned here. Both are substantially Norman, Bayton retaining its drum-shaped Norman font and Mamble having an unfortunate excrescence on the north side built of bricks, the lower courses of about 1560 and the upper of about 1800. This is the Blount Chapel and a grisly cadaver on a family tomb is a reminder of the transitoriness of human life and family fortunes.

On the west side of the river as we approach Tenbury we must spare a line or two for four churches. Stoke Bliss has an Early English chancel and south aisle and a drum-shaped Norman font. The pulpit and reading desk are Laudian. Kyre Wyard stands hard by the great house of Kyre Park which is now a home for spastics. The house is rather a jumble with a tiny bit of medieval work, a seventeenth-century door case, much eighteenth-century work and a rather disappointing interior. There is a 1754 staircase and another which may be Elizabethan. The outbuildings, including a Jacobean brick barn and a circular medieval dovecote have considerable charm, and the grounds are supposed to have been laid out by Lancelot Brown. The church again is basically Norman and has a few interesting features including a fine mural painting of a saint of early fourteenth-century date near the south-west window of the chapel. A very recent addition is perhaps one of the most remarkable things in the church; it is the Harmon memorial, a shining example of a neo-Baroque tablet, and a cordial for flagging spirits which are encouraged to believe that the age of exquisite craftsmanship and of generosity in setting up beautiful things in remote churches is not entirely extinguished.

Before we reach the end of this spoke at Tenbury we are left only with the two Hanleys. Hanley Child has the nave and chancel and remains of a west tower which fell in 1864; it was built in 1807. Hanley William is of Norman origin, built in red sandstone and tufa. So we emerge from this territory of small hedge churches, surprisingly remote even in this twentieth century but rewarding in architectural details for those who have patience to search for them and arrive at a place of some consequence and of strong antiquarian lineage.

Tenbury would no doubt rather be known as 'the town in the orchard' (a remark attributed to Queen Victoria) than 'the spa that failed'. Undoubtedly it must have been a place of strategic importance in British, Roman and Welsh Border conflicts, but to associate it very closely with Caractacus and even to point out to us his grave we can only attribute to the over-exuberance of local patriotism. But of the lusciousness of its apple orchards there can be no doubt for here again we are in a heart of the cider country. Indeed, the same local historian says—'The fact is that cider in the Tenbury neighbourhood is not merely a popular beverage: it has been for generations a part of the life and culture of the people.'

The town contains some fine old houses and inns of half-timbered construction, but the church, apart from its monuments is a little disappointing. It is of unusual width and is at least the third structure to stand upon a site which is as old as Anglo-Saxon Christianity, whose converts would be baptised in the neighbouring river. It was the work of Henry Woodyer in 1865. The monuments include a fine Easter sepulchre and canopy of the fourteenth century which covers a miniature effigy of a cross-legged knight holding his heart; no doubt a location of 'heart burial' as at Bredon. Parts of an Anglo-Saxon cross shaft are a reminder of the earliest Christian associations of this place.

But the dilapidated Pump Room in the centre of the town is a curious reminiscence of a 'might have been'. A spring of mineral waters was discovered accidentally in 1839 and brine water, said to contain a larger amount of saline matter than the springs of Chelten-ham and Leamington, issued from a massive stratum of old Red Sand-stone. A small red brick bath house first, and later larger premises, were added. The Pump Room advertised itself as a 'spa for middling and working classes' and offered 'every convenience at the lowest possible price'. As late as 1931 the local historian was speculating that 'some hydros and new residential houses built on the higher banks round the town might solve the question and make Tenbury a second Droitwich'. It was not to be. 'The middling and working classes' had neither time nor means to lavish on the sort of treatment their richer neighbours could afford at Droitwich or Malvern. The Pump Room closed in 1939, the wells were filled in and the dilapi-dated building now does whatever useful service it can, including the place for the sale of Women's Institute produce.

Henry Woodyer, who was a very considerable Victorian architect, also built in 1856 St. Michael's College, two miles from the town. This is a notable pile of neo-Gothic buildings housing the music school built at the expense of the Revd. Sir Frederick Gore Ouseley. The College, happily, still flourishes, housing a preparatory school and promoting the production of first-rate Church music which is presented at two choral services each day. The services which are open to the public deserve to be better known and patronised. In the College library here is the score of the *Messiah* from which Handel conducted its first performance.

At Tenbury we lose our Worcester Teme to Shropshire. Enthusi-asts who may be so minded can pursue it further, a delightful and rewarding excursion tracking it to its source, as the present writer once found. The journey would take us through the great medieval stronghold of Ludlow, through Leintwardine and across the Welsh border through Newtown. Then, passing through villages with such bewitching names as Beguildy and Felindre you would find, if you were energetic enough to tramp over those boggy Welsh uplands a place where a spring emerges from rough turf, quickly becomes a substantial trickle, then a mountain stream before it broadens out into the wide river flowing through Shropshire and Worcestershire to join the Severn near Powick Bridge.

The valley along which we have followed it is surely one of the most beautiful and unspoilt scenic expanses in the country. Industry scarcely touches it and it is away from the best known and most used tourist routes. Bungaloid development is very sparse and environmental worries about conservation seem a long way off. Treasures of architecture and antiquarian interest line its banks and its waters are a joy to fishermen. In spite of the hazards of the twentieth-century industrial scene we are not unduly worried about the integrity of our lovely valley. It seems hardly likely that exploitation here would be feasible on a scale to make it worthwhile and it is sufficiently loved by those who know it to make them defend its amenities to the utmost of their powers.

CHAPTER THREE

South-West to Malvern
and Beyond

We turn our backs on the hub and follow a south-west spoke to
Malvern and the now disafforested country of Malvern Chase which
lies beyond it. Leaving Worcester we travel via St. John's towards the
A449 and traversing the suburban sprawl which demonstrates the
ability of modern builders to turn out new houses with the repetitive
accuracy of the sausage machine, we reach Powick Bridge. Travellers
with extra-sensory perception may catch an echo of the clash of arms
between Royalist and Parliamentary forces at this point. The
majority will pass on rapidly to the centre of the village, taking care
with the road system which involves a roundabout and a gyratory
at this point. A little outside Worcester opposite Bennett's Dairies,
they will already have negotiated successfully a piece of traffic
experimentation which partakes more of the nature of an archipelago
than an island. But having arrived safely at Powick where the church,
a large one, stands on high ground safely overlooking the frequently
flooded river-side meadows, they should not miss this church clearly
marked by its stately Perpendicular tower. It dates from the twelfth
and thirteenth centuries and the nave and transepts, though domin-
antly of a later and largely Perpendicular period, are obviously
following the lines of an earlier plan, for each transept retains a
Norman window. A striking feature here is the elegant monument
by Thomas Scheemakers to Mrs. Russell, who died in 1786. The
young mother, who favours a somewhat revealing type of dress is,
on the sarcophagus, portrayed more decently clad, as the situation
would seem to require, teaching her child music. The instruments
are there, too, delightfully portrayed; altogether a most charming

composition. In the churchyard the Wheeley Lea table tomb, with its inlet panels of white marble funerary sculpture, is at least respect-worthy.

Victorian enthusiasts must travel along the Upton road to Callow End and look at one of the best of our neo-Gothic buildings in the County. This is Stanbrook Abbey built by E. W. Pugin between 1878 and 1880. *In a Great Tradition* is the title of the story of these Benedictines of Stanbrook written as a tribute to their Abbess, Dame Laurentia MacLachlan. It is well named. Stanbrook finds its origin in a community of English nuns who founded a house at Cambrai in the penal era of 1623. They were evicted by Revolutionary French forces in 1793 and endured a time of much hardship and danger until they decided that the order should return to England in 1795. For 12 years they were in Liverpool where they conducted a school; then in 1807 were allowed to rent Salford Hall, a fine Tudor mansion beyond Evesham over the Warwickshire border, which still stands. At last in 1835, after Catholic Emancipation, came a home of their own when the Stanbrook estate was purchased. Dame Laurentia (1866–1953) was a woman of commanding personality, deep scholarship and a wide capacity for friendship. Sir Ivor Atkins, the musician, the scholarly Canon J. M. Wilson with whom she worked on Cathedral manuscripts and music books, for she was a pioneer in the restoration of the Gregorian chant, and Sir Sydney Cockerell, the noted bibliophile, were amongst her friends. Most striking of all was her communication with George Bernard Shaw, some of whose long and surprising letters are preserved in the book *In a Great Tradition*. Shaw wrote, 'The thought of Stanbrook is a delight to me. It is one of my holy places.'

We return to Powick and follow the main Malvern road. Powick Hospital, a somewhat sinister name in Worcestershire ears, is on our left-hand side. It is a gaunt complex of buildings dating from 1852 and nowadays should be a reminder of the fact that the treatment of the mentally sick is far more compassionate and skilful and hopeful than at the time when it was first built.

We are in Beauchamp territory now, the demesne of the Lygon family which has played an important role not only in County affairs and in the shaping of modern Malvern but also in Parliamentary and national affairs. Their home is at Madresfield, a small village reached down a road to the left at the Newland corner. The Court is vast, the encircling moat has masonry of fifteenth-century date and a portion of the south front is Elizabethan, but the majority of the building is by P. C. Hardwick and dates from 1863. It is a skilful piece of work, succeeding by its variety in heights and directions and its purposeful shunning of all symmetry. Inside, there are bits and pieces of antique furnishings and chimney pieces brought from other houses and built into the structure. The chapel has a special interest, being a complete exercise in *art nouveau* of 1902 and given by Countess Beauchamp to her husband, the seventh earl, as a wedding present, a circumstance which seems to have been adapted by Evelyn Waugh in one of his most famous novels.

The gardens contain vast walls of towering yew hedge and Victorian architects are represented here by Norman Shaw, who restored the circular brick dovecote in 1867 and built the west and north lodges. It has been asserted that C. F. A. Voysey built a pair of lodge cottages in 1901, but Lord Beauchamp has no record of Voysey having worked at Madresfield; indeed, according to Mr. Brandon-Jones, who is our expert on Voysey studies, it appears that Bannut Tree Farm House at Castlemorton is the only example of that architect's work in the County, though he lists the War Memorial at Malvern Wells as Voysey's. But not very far away, over the hill in Herefordshire, on Jubilee Drive, is Perrycroft, one of the most important examples of his work, a house now in the useful keeping of the Birmingham Battalion of the Boys' Brigade as a holiday hostel.

Madresfield Court is open to the public only on special occasions. The parish church by F. Preedy who was responsible for much Worcestershire restoration and building and whom we shall often meet on our travels, is a competent Victorian building in late thirteenth-century style and contains modest memorials to the Beauchamp family.

We return to Newland, which is a place of some significance, being one of the medieval chapelries out of which the modern Malvern grew. Part of the fourteenth-century half-timbered chapel of St. Leonard is still to be found encased in the complex of nineteenth-century buildings and used at one time as a mortuary. For in 1864 came the building of the Newland church we now see, part of a remarkable collection of buildings which are a memorial to both the piety and romanticism of religious Victorian aristocrats. In the '60s came the erection of houses for 12 or more poor men and women formerly employed in agriculture; in 1889 came the Lygon Almshouses and in 1900, endowed by the Revd. G. C. White, the St. Barnabas houses for retired clergy. It was all a singular idea born perhaps of the cult of revived medievalism, initiated by Sir Walter Scott and nurtured by the picturesque piety of the Catholic Revival. Lord Shrewsbury and A. W. N. Pugin were its exponents under the Roman obedience at Alton Towers; Disraeli knew all about it when he made his hero Coningsby visit his friend Mr. Lyle at Beaumanoir and saw the procession of pilgrims, certified by the almoner, and making their way to receive the squire's benefactions at the hand of the steward and 'blessing the bell that sounded from the tower of St. Genevieve'. This mock-medievalism of the Victorians is a curious psychological phenomenon which deserves to be more closely studied. Here at Newland something of its Anglican counterpart still survived, at any rate until fairly recently, when the pensioners in their distinctive gowns attended the Sunday Eucharist in the Victorian church and the floating clouds of incense and the tinkling bells still commemorated the gesture of seigniorial piety to recreate a neo-Catholic medievalism which just failed to come off.

The component parts of this architectural complex, though not entirely satisfactory, are a gallant attempt to provide a habitation for this curious bit of Victorian idealism; and the church, with its paired marble columns, its elaborate oriel window in the west wall through which sick members of the community could view and share the proceedings, and above all with its most important spirit frescoes designed by Gambier Parry and carried out by Clayton and Bell, is a period piece of highest importance.

So we continue through the shopping centre of Malvern Link, across the railway line near the station, on along the main road flanked on the left by the wide spreading Link Common and on the right by schools housed in handsome Victorian villas, until at Link Top we take the sharp left turn which brings us soon to the centre of the town which we call Great Malvern.

Malvern is a palimpsest and it is a fascinating exercise to uncover the various strata which through the centuries have overlaid one another to form the beautiful town which now exists. First, of course, is the massive range of ancient Silurian rock which stretches north–south from Suckley to Holly Bush and forms the western boundary of Worcestershire and Herefordshire. Indeed you could scarcely be said to have lost the Malverns when you go on beyond the north hill and explore Ankerdine and Berrow and Woodbury and Abberley which are part of the same system, some of the oldest rock in the world. But the Herefordshire Beacon and the Worcestershire Beacon and the North Hill are particularly Malvern's own and the essence of Malvern is that it is a string of village communities which encircle the hills. And when you note Holy Well and St. Ann's Well marked in antique lettering on the map you begin to find the reason which made Malvern take its origin as a favoured place. Bronze Age and Iron Age burials and remains have been found along the range and the excellence of the water that sprang from the hills in many more places than those two famous wells must have been known to the hill dwellers from very early times. The importance of the woodland which covered the area as a Royal Chase made it jealously guarded, as many medieval lawsuits demonstrate, and it was not until dis-afforestation and enclosure made a settled agriculture possible that town life had an opportunity to develop. The whole story of this development is brilliantly told in Brian Smith's *History of Malvern*.

Much of this early period in the overlaying strata is now beyond our observation, but we can still see extensive evidence of the time when the great Priory dominated the community, indeed, for the most part *was* the community. Discounting the very unsure stories of a flight from Deerhurst when the Danes sacked that monastery and of Anglo-Saxon monks settling here before the Conquest we are on much firmer ground when we ascribe the foundation to Aldwin, a monk, about 1085. The sturdy Norman arcade of the nave seems to echo Wulfstan's building at Worcester and it is possible that a substantial new home may have been erected then for a small company of monks who were leading a conventual life in a simple way near by. From the start the great royal foundation at West-minster seems to have exercised a strong influence at Malvern and later quarrels which arose with the Bishop about unsatisfactory states of affairs at Malvern sometimes resolved themselves into conflicts between the Bishop of Worcester and the Abbot of Westminster. Until the Dissolution Malvern was content to be regarded as a cell of Westminster.

But superimposed on the Norman base, much of what we see now is the remaking of the Priory church in the fifteenth century. Between 1400 and 1460, very shortly before the Reformation, the great building assumed much of its present form. The Perpendicular style took its origin in Gloucester and there is much in Malvern to remind us of Gloucester, suggesting even that some of the work here may be by the same masons. The tower particularly is obviously copied from Gloucester and apart from the Norman arcades retained to provide the basic stability it may be said that the fifteenth-century Perpendicular builders gave us a new church from end to end. On 30 July 1460, John Carpenter, Bishop of Worcester, reconsecrated the renewed church and its seven altars. But in less than one hundred years, before the end of 1539, the Priory of Great Malvern had been 'surrendered and dissolved' and the work of destruction begun.

So as one steps down from the north-west door and surveys the length of the church from west to east one enters upon an almost breathtaking experience. Standing as it were in a many-coloured jewelled lantern one can only wonder at the amazing good fortune that so much was spared for the inspiration of later ages. Canon Anthony Deane, who was vicar here from 1909 to 1914 and who has written one of the best accounts of the Priory says, very justly, 'There are ancient churches which strike one chiefly as being places of archaeological interest. There are others, and Great Malvern Priory Church is of the number, which stir deeper feelings and within them seems to brood the very Peace of God.' The present writer would re-echo those sentiments and if he were allowed a single lapse into the language of mystical theology, would affirm that he knows no building more potent in raising a sense of the numinous than this inspired shrine of Malvern Priory.

Again, the marvel of the thing is that so much that is beautiful survived. It was touch and go. Speedily the conventual buildings were swept away. The chapter house, the dormitory, the refectory all went. What was the cloister garth is now part of the modern Abbey Hotel garden coming right up to the south side of the church. The abbey gateway remained; it looks like fifteenth-century work, but what we see now is so excessively restored that it is largely a Victorian piece of work. All these 'superfluous buildings', thus demolished, were sold for £9.8.4. Next came the church's turn. The Lady Chapel and the small south transept were destroyed, the lead from the church roof stripped and sold. Then came the miracle. The townspeople of Malvern, led by John Pope, stepped in and offered to buy the Priory Church from the Crown to replace their own parish church of St. Thomas. How often we have seen incredulous smiles when the figure of £20 which they paid for it has been mentioned. But if you multiply that sum by something like 50 to get some idea of present-day values you may think that there was some pretty heavy sacrifice involved on the part of what were probably a handful of poor villagers in order to save the lovely thing. But it was done and their sacrifice has preserved Malvern Priory for us today. The repairs to the initial damage appear to have been a botched-up job, the best that a poverty-stricken community could do. There is an intriguing note that in 1549 the vicar had to sell a chalice 'to paye the churche debtes and to repare the churche'. There might be a precedent here for those who are looking for ammunition in the current acrimonious debate as to whether the Church is entitled to sell its 'treasures on earth' in order to pay the astronomical costs of modern restoration.

That is not the end of the good luck story. In succeeding centuries scandalous neglect and injudicious restoration almost did what the Dissolution just failed to do. To that small band of inhabitants the maintenance of such a vast building must have been, understandably, an almost impossible burden. By the end of the eighteenth century it had reached a very bad state of repair. The churchyard was a playground, the Jesus Chapel was a pigeon loft, the roof was crumbling, the walls and floor damp and sometimes flooded and ivy, even within the building, was allowed to pursue its corrosive course. In 1809 and 1812 some attempt at improvement was made, but it was very inadequate. The Revd. Henry Card, the vicar in 1815, took the restoration work more seriously, but some of it was unsuitable and injudicious. Embellishments and classical furnishings were introduced instead of vital roof repairs, but not until 1860 during the incumbency of the Revd. S. Fisk was a truly capable architect employed and luckily it was not too late for Sir Gilbert Scott to carry out the complete reparation, which if somewhat drastic for some tastes and lacking the conservative restraint which it would no doubt have received today, gave us a building in which there is singularly little to criticise.

Numerous excellent guide books will supply the visitor with the information about Malvern Priory which there is no room to furnish here. Three features, however, must be stressed; the glass, the misericords and the tiles. The extensive array of stained glass in the Priory windows is one of the finest collections of its kind that survives in cathedral or church in England today. In spite of wanton damage and some ill arrangement due to the ignorance of restorers we have a panoply of inspired craftsmanship dating from the period 1460–1485 when the art of stained glass making in this country probably reached its peak. The antiquarian Habington, and observers in the eighteenth and nineteenth centuries, have left us records of the glass as it appeared in their day, so we know fairly well where the original makers intended to place it. Much of it has subsequently become jumbled and misplaced but a careful scrutiny, preferably with field glasses, gives one a fair idea of the subjects and sequences, and detailed information can be sought in Canon Anthony Deane's book and by the more enthusiastic searcher in the massive and scholarly work of G. McN. Rushworth and the shorter though quite excellent and well-illustrated book by L. A. Hamand which is based on it.

There are 24 original misericords or monks' seats, 22 of them heavily carved underneath, 12 illustrated miscellaneous scenes such as a mummer's mask, a merman with a mirror, a sick man in bed and a woman driving away a demon with a pair of bellows. The other 12 represent roughly the occupations of the seasons, a favourite subject with this sort of carving, but the sequences of subjects appear to be much disturbed and mixed.

Finally, the tiles, and it is important to examine carefully those that cover the semi-circular apse wall. These make up most of the collection of medieval tiles, and those on the sides of the sanctuary

14 (*opposite above*) *Malvern Priory – Perpendicular: the genuine article and nineteenth-century imitation*
15 (*below*) *Little Malvern Court – Recusant stronghold*

and the floors of the church are a nineteenth-century imitation. But the genuine medieval tiles, more than a thousand of them, are a remarkable and extensive collection and remind us that in the fifteenth century Malvern Priory had a famous reputation for its tile manufacture and supplied churches near and far, not only with any sort of tile but with the precise designs which we find here in the Priory. A kiln was discovered on Priory land about 1830. It was 35 feet in length and was buried 7 feet below the surface of the ground. The patterns are, for the most part, armorial bearings, the crowned sacred monogram, traceried panels, symbols of the Passion, floreated designs and even one or two didactic inscriptions. They are mostly of mid-fifteenth-century date, 1453 and 1456, though a few are of an earlier date, belonging to the fourteenth century.

We have by no means exhausted the charms of Malvern when we emerge from the Priory. Having thus examined the monastic stratum in the town's history let us now go in search of the other layers which have been superimposed on it. The seventeenth and eighteenth centuries seem to have added nothing to the expansion of the town; and this was a pity when lovely Palladian mansions were going up in the surrounding country and handsome Georgian façades were adorning streets of other towns. Enclosures and hill paths and some roads may represent some progress, but the truth is that up to about 1800 Malvern remained an obscure and poverty-stricken village.

And then came the water cure and the town blossomed. It is quite wrong to think that Dr. John Wall invented the water cure. The healing qualities of Malvern water were probably appreciated from primitive times and the existence of curative wells may have been one reason for the establishment and growth of the Priory in this place. Certainly in the seventeenth and eighteenth centuries we have documentary evidence of persons visiting the wells for water cures and there was a little accommodation for visitors. Abbey House and Well House were taking people and they are the forerunners of Malvern's later hotel popularity. But it is in the first two decades of the nineteenth century that development gets under way and we have plentiful archaeological evidence for the fact. The Foley Arms, the classical library, Edith Lodge and Oriel House are attributed

16 (*opposite*) *Ripple Church – Misericords: 'The Sun' and 'Labours Of the Months'*

to Samuel and John Deykes, the town's first farsighted building pioneers; and with the advance of the century building went on rapidly.

It is a fascinating exercise to examine carefully the row of substantial villas which continues along the Worcester road beyond the Foley Arms. These have been assigned to John Deykes and are a remarkable symposium of early nineteenth-century taste, ranging from the neo-classical to the Gothic as it was understood in the 1830s.

Other amenities arrived by the middle of the century. *A Guide to Malvern with observations on the Air and Waters and a short description of the most remarkable objects in the neighbourhood* gives us a view of the waxing town at this period. It speaks of recently built hotels, the Royal Kent, Coburg and Foley Hotel, its title proudly expanded in honour of the much-cherished memory of the young Princess Victoria who with her mother, the Duchess of Kent, stayed in Malvern in 1830. This hotel and the Belle Vue are described as generally crowded with rank and fashion during the season. And in their train came the 'Boarding and Lodging Houses', like Montrose House about which 'Miss Bullock respectfully informs families and visitors to Great Malvern that she has erected commodious Premises situated in the very best part of that delightful village (*sic*) commanding its extensive and beautifully picturesque scenery, and which she has conveniently fitted up . . . Miss Bullock begs to assure families who may favor her with their commands, that every energy shall be used to promote their comfort and satisfaction'. Miss Bullock was the first swallow of a bounteous summer. Montrose House happily still survives near the Church Street end of Graham Road, but has graduated from a 'Boarding and Lodging House' to carry on a dignified trade as the Montrose Hotel.

But we have reached the era of the popularity of the water cure and the *Guide* goes on to inform us that Hydropathic Establishments upon a large scale have been established for some years, conducted by Doctors Wilson and Gully. It boasts of the Library, a handsome modern building in the Italian style and a Reading Room and Bazaar. Private education has already begun to raise its blessed head and at Spring Villa Miss Harling provides 'the comforts of home' along with 'instruction in every branch of a refined education'. At

Pomona House the very appropriately named Misses Clinnick pay 'particular attention to the health and moral training of pupils'. Dismissed more briefly, there are two charity schools and a Dispensary.

It is these doctors, Wilson and Gully, who have initiated much of this new prosperity for Malvern and they must certainly be noticed. It was they who in 1845 built at a cost of £18,000 the Priessnitz Hotel as a centre for the adaptation of the hydropathic methods of Wilson's mentor, Vincenz Priessnitz of Graefenburg in Silesia, to the amenities and scenic advantages of Malvern in Worcestershire. Details of the water cure, which are fully recorded, must be read elsewhere. But it would seem that its barbarous methods, with the wrapping in wet sheets and the drinking of copious draughts, were cheerfully endured by its Spartan votaries. Whether it amounted to anything much more than a rigid dietary and strenuous exercise for over-fed and over-indulged voluptuaries is a matter for speculation. Anyhow it was a heinous crime for any of the patients to be detected in the streets of Malvern with a surreptitious bag of buns. But in spite of the critical opposition of more conservative doctors like Sir Charles Hastings, bred at Martley and now living at Barnard's Green house and founder of the British Medical Association, the strenuous regime of the water cure did not lack its devotees. Gladstone, Macaulay, Dickens, Carlyle, Florence Nightingale and many other giants of the Victorian scene testified to benefits received and the doctors, particularly Gully, made a very good thing, financially, out of it. Eventually there developed an estrangement between the partners and the later years of Dr. Gully were much clouded by his association with the leading character in a notorious poison trial later in the century with whom he had formed a romantic association while she was one of his patients at Malvern. The story has been fully told and the former Priory House and Stokefield House in Graham Road, perhaps the most gracious of all our Regency-style houses, figure in it.

So in the extensive Victorian building which went on in Malvern for the rest of the century we meet the next archaeological layer and deeply impressive is that stage in our town's history. These houses are deserving of the most careful study by enthusiasts of architecture and much careful work has been done on them by Miss P. G. Mann and other local writers. Little can be said here, but a walk round Avenue Road, Priory Road, Orchard Road and other of the thoroughfares in the centre of the town is a most rewarding experience. Building covenants enforced by the ground landlords, particularly the Foley Estate, ensured dignified and spacious positioning of the houses most of which stand in wide gardens surrounded by tree-lined streets. The characteristic local hard granite, with its jig-saw patterns from which many of the houses and walls are built, came from numerous small local quarries. Some tastes find this material heavy and forbidding; to others it is part of the particular Malvern charm. But by the end of the century this Malvern stone had for the most part been superseded by brick and slates, and even yellow-glazed brick with terra cotta dressings supply some of us with habitations which we are assured make up in durability what they lack in aesthetic appeal. One house only may be suggested for special inspection, The Priory, adjoining the Gardens, and now the council house, was the work of the Haddon Brothers, Malvern architects and the designs were exhibited in the Royal Academy of 1874. Exclusive of grates, chimney pieces, parquetry, dado panelling and all decorative works and stabling, it cost £10,650. The intricate carving by Forsyth of Worcester is superb; it is unlikely that such dwelling houses will ever be built again. Long may Malvern preserve and respect them.

A word must be said about educational establishments, for Malvern has been a great place for schools since the days of the Misses Harling and Clinnick. Malvern College is a school of some eminence. It was founded in 1862, its original building was by Charles F. Hansom in 1863, and since then it has gathered round it a congerie of buildings of successive periods exhibiting the work of such celebrated architects as Blomfield who did the chapel in 1897 and Sir Aston Webb who gave us what Pevsner calls the best building of the College, the Memorial Library in 1924. Inevitably, with the expansion of science teaching, the building work still goes on. Then for the girls there is the gargantuan College in Avenue Road. This started life as the Station Hotel and was built in the Gothic taste by E. W. Elmslie in 1861. Those who like the modern idiom will be pleased by Maurice Jones' and Tom Burrough's new boarding house, Hatfield, which with its many zig-zag façades provides an unusual personal privacy in the girls' dormitories. Numerous prosperous Preparatory Schools are scattered round the town, housed for the most part in elegant Victorian villas. Public education gradually catches up, for Malvern, ever mindful of the education of children from other parts, seems content to have left the education of its own young to the churches and charitable bodies. It has never possessed its own Grammar School. But times change and in the Chase School and the Dyson Perrins School, which seems likely to be the only Church of England Aided Comprehensive School in the Worcester Diocese, the town will possess two modern 'Comprehensives' of which it may be justly proud.

Malvern has many well kept and prosperous churches and chapels. G. E. Street, who is not particularly well represented in the County, though his ancestors at one time inhabited Greyfriars in Worcester has two churches here, St. Peter's Cowleigh and St. James, West Malvern, which are each Victorian period gems. St. Matthias, Malvern Link, was started by Sir Gilbert Scott in 1844 but altered out of recognition by F. W. Hunt in 1880–81. It is a very large church and has long sustained a lively Anglo-Catholic tradition. It has a finely carved rood and the lower panels of the rood screen are exquisitely painted in figure studies by a religious of the nearby Convent of the Holy Name. Those who delight in the woodwork of Thompson of Leyburn and like to find mice in church will enjoy his parclose screen at the east end of the north aisle. This appears to be the only example of Thompson's work in Worcestershire. Perhaps the most exciting piece of modern church architecture is Walter Tapper's Ascension Church of 1903 at Malvern Link. Built of Guiting stone and stuccoed brick, it soars to a roof of great height with the chancel rib-vaulted and the nave with a tunnel vault. Separating them is Bainbridge Reynolds' fine metal screen. The Convent of the Holy Name, also at the Link, has an extensive complex of buildings which houses one of the most prosperous Orders in the Church of England. Its chapel, of 1903, by Comper, white-walled and with much colour and gilding and with stained glass by Comper, is quite awe-inspiring.

97

So we come to the top stratum of the palimpsest which is modern Malvern and that to the visitor will be sufficiently obvious to require little direction here. The Winter Garden in Grange Road dates from 1884 and the adjoining theatres, live and cinema, provide excellent entertainment. There was a time when the Malvern Festival was one of the principal cultural events in the Midlands. It began in 1929 and continued until the Second World War and under the management of Sir Barry Jackson achieved such eminence as to stage 19 of Shaw's plays including the first production of *The Apple Cart* and *In Good King Charles's Golden Days*. The gardens, which sweep downwards from the theatres and Winter Garden to the swimming pool, are bright with carefully tended flower beds and tall trees afford shade for the deck chairs spread out beneath them. The Priory Gardens on a sunny summer afternoon are indeed a pleasant place.

The last and most surprising development in Malvern is a matter of recent history and is really a national story. In 1942 the radar research stations arrived in the town. It is true to say that the 2,500 scientists and staff who were quartered in Malvern College which had to move to Harrow School were one of the principal factors in winning the war in the air. Nor did this astonishing episode in the history of Malvern come to an end with the war; the Royal Radar Establishment, which received permanent buildings in 1955 provides one of the most important schools of electronics in the country. All these newcomers have brought the population of Malvern to somewhere near the 25,000 mark. So when William Langland now looks down from some celestial observation post upon his 'fair field full of folk' he finds it replenished with its native townspeople, its hundreds of retired immigrants who have been finding Malvern a very pleasant place in which to end their days since Victorian times, and with a new sort of people young and old whose keen scientific brains add an entirely new dimension to the town's extensive cultural life. It is unlikely that his Piers Plowman would be displeased.

It is time now to take our leave of these great granite hills whose rhythmic contours have inspired music both vocal and instrumental. When Jenny Lind, the Swedish Nightingale came to live at Wynd's Point she was as ready to serve and delight Malvern townspeople with her exquisite voice as she had been the national audience who hung upon her unbelievable notes. In a different manifestation of rhythm, Edward Elgar, who had three homes in Malvern, composed his *Dream of Gerontius* and his *Enigma Variations*. It was without doubt from these ancient hills that he derived much of his inspiration as an unforgettable documentary taught us some years ago, on the television.

So, having lifted our eyes to the hills we must now turn our backs upon them and pursue our journey eastwards. To the south end of the range is the almost self-contained village of Malvern Wells which contains one of the Malvern's oldest hotels which dates from the beginning of the nineteenth century, the Essington, and a church of 1836 in the early experimental lancet window Gothic style with the usual nave, short chancel and transepts of that time. If the traveller had time to stray over the hills a little way into the neighbouring county he might find himself among the few remaining fragments of a very remarkable house, the vanished home of two celebrated women, Hope End. This was the bizarre oriental-styled home of Edward Moulton Barrett, perhaps better known for his residence in Wimpole Street. Here surprisingly, the children and father lived a completely affectionate family life. In a fragmentary diary entitled *E.B.B.* kept for a short time by Elizabeth in 1831/32 we read much of her visits to Malvern Wells to an old blind scholar, a Mr. Boyd, for whom she had an obsessive and jealous affection, at a fine eighteenth-century house with bow windows which still stands. Near by is the Hornyold Arms opened about 1825 and formerly called the Admiral Benbow. Ruby, the house that Elizabeth so often visited, was named after one of the ships in the admiral's fleet. It was a sad year for Elizabeth, for Papa's financial affairs were in low water and she knew that her beloved Hope End would certainly have to be sold. Its purchaser was Thomas Heywood, member of a noted Manchester banking family and the second celebrated woman who lived at and loved Hope End was his daughter Mary, who, in her married name of Mary Sumner is known to innumerable good Anglican women as the founder of the Mothers' Union. Hope End was eventually burnt down but sufficient has survived in the stable block with its dome and minarets to show what a curious oriental architectural fantasy the whole building must have been.

In the graveyard of the Roman Catholic church of St. Wulfstan, a building of 1862 by B. Bucknall, Sir Edward Elgar is buried.

Turning a little to the east from the main road at Malvern Wells, the medieval enthusiast receives a little bonus. This is Little Malvern Priory, not to be compared with its grandiose neighbour two miles away but an interesting monastic enclave of which more in fact of the conventual buildings survive. It was founded about 1125 and Aldwin of Great Malvern was probably responsible for it. While Great Malvern had a strong connection with Westminster it was made clear from the start that Little Malvern's dependence was to be upon Worcester, and so it continued to the end, with considerable advantage to the Little Priory. It was never of much importance. At its peak, in 1323, it housed about 12 monks but on the eve of the Dissolution it fell as low as five and by 1480 it was almost derelict. Bishop Alcock of Worcester certainly effected some small repair and rebuilding on the tower and choir but the nave remained ruinous. So what we see now is the truncated chancel of the Priory. In 1539 the buildings were leased from the Crown to Henry Russell and sufficient were retained to form a house for the local squire, which continues to this day. Little Malvern Court embodies the west range of the cloisters and includes a magnificent hall which was probably the Prior's Refectory. A most extensive and costly restoration has recently been completed and the public are admitted to this part of the Court on Wednesdays in the summer months. The hall is supported on an undercroft of stone which dates from the twelfth century, but the fine timbered roof with its five bays with trefoil openings in the apex of the roof is probably part of Bishop Alcock's restoration of the buildings in 1480. There are two small rooms at the west end of the hall, one with a stone fireplace and the other with its original floor boards which are contemporary and may have been guest rooms.

A splendid collection of Eucharistic vestments is also displayed, a reminder that the Court has always been a Recusant stronghold and that the Papal allegiance was maintained throughout penal times and mass said in the house for a handful of neighbours who persevered in keeping the Roman Catholic faith alive in the Malvern area. The church of St. Wulfstan replaced this domestic chapel in

1862. The tradition is still cherished that the Court is the scene of the opening chapter of J. H. Shorthouse's *John Inglesant*.

Incidentally, as we leave the churchyard, it is worth noting one of the most comely church notice boards we have ever come across.

Continuing eastward to the cross-roads at Welland we find the church of St. James, designed by J. W. Hugall in 1875 and built in the Malvern 'jig-saw' idiom; its east window is probably by Hardman and it has one south aisle window by Kempe. Welland Court is a well-proportioned Georgian house. To the north is Guarlford, its Commissioners' type of church, also with Malvern walling, by Thomas Bellamy in 1843. Next come Hanley Swan and Hanley Castle, the former with one of Sir Gilbert Scott's few Worcestershire churches, with circular clerestory windows and a good east window with five graduated lancet lights. The reredos is the joint work of Powell, and Clayton and Bell and the contemporary tiling is good.

At Hanley Swan, too, the Roman Catholic church of 1846 is by Charles Hansom and its furnishings by A. W. Pugin, one of the few examples of his work in the County. There was no lack of money when this church was built, as so often happened with Catholic congregations at that time. The local landowning family of Hornyold was Catholic and contributed generously, so the architectural details and reredos are rich and good. It is possible that the presbytery may be Pugin's work; it is very much in his style.

Hanley Castle is a much more important place. The castle was the seat of administration for Malvern Chase and was built between 1206 and 1213 by King John. Occupied later by the Earls of Gloucester and Warwick it fell into decay in Henry VII's reign according to his policy of breaking the stronghold power of a belligerent aristocracy and today only three sides of a moat mark the site of what was once an important fortress. But the medieval church survives with Norman fragments, a north aisle of about 1300 and a central tower, chancel and north chapel built of brick in 1674. The chapel windows indicate that the Gothic tradition was still lingering until the end of the seventeenth century; indeed, as we know, it never entirely faded out of the English architectural development. There are Lechmere monuments, of course, for we are in the territory of the Lechmeres here, one of the historic County families. They still live at Severn

End, near by, a house largely destroyed by fire in 1896 but skilfully restored. At one time they lived at Rhydd Court in Guarlford parish, a house of no particular architectural distinction by Brandon, of 1863, but understandably later elected to return to the home of their ancestors. The Court now does useful service under the County as a special school for boys. Hanley Castle also has almshouses of 1600 and one of the few country grammar schools, founded in 1544. Its ancient status has recently been altered in modern educational re-arrangements and with the admission of girl pupils.

Our next stop is at Upton-on-Severn, a town set in what a writer calls 'Constable-like' country and possessing considerable historical associations. Upton thrived when Severn river traffic was at its most prosperous; its peak was probably the second half of the eighteenth century when river trade was enormous and the town was a posting house for busy roads. It played a small part in the Civil War, in 1643, when the Parliamentarians were rebuffed, and again in 1651 when Cromwell sent Lambert to occupy Upton and his men managed, as we have seen, to cross the ruined bridge on a plank carelessly left across the broken arches by the defenders. The Royalists were driven out of the town and the Scots army retreated towards Worcester.

A bridge of 1853 replaced this one that was 250 years older and then, in 1939, the present handsome structure was built. The liability of the river to flood has been a constant hazard in the development of Upton's story. The town has known three churches. Of the first two, near the bridge, little remains. The lower stages of the tower which still stands, with the lowered walls of the later nave, date from the fourteenth century. The local writer, 'E.M.L.', who turns out to be Mrs. Lawson the wife of the rector and herself no inconsiderable local historian, in 1869 described the tower as disfigured by a mean cupola and the church as 'altogether unbeautiful, judged by the architectural notions of this generation.' She waxes wrathful about the total destruction of the old church and the replacement by the building she knew, in 1757. 'All that can be said in praise of the church,' she continues, 'is that it has a very wide span of roof and that it is not devoid of a certain picturesqueness when viewed from a distance.' Faint praise indeed, but each generation is rarely enthusiastic about the architectural achievements of its predecessor. Actually, from a print hanging in the vestry, it looks a rather fine Georgian church of a type which would be far more appreciated today. It was by John Willoughby of Worcester and its cupola was by Anthony Keck, who designed the original Worcester Infirmary, and its builder was P. H. Sheward whose name also appears on a tablet as the builder of the present rectory. In fact, the medieval tower, crowned by the rather delicate Adam-like cupola, skilfully coloured in recent restoration is an entirely delightful and satisfactory feature of the riverscape. Upton people are to be congratulated on its preservation.

But perhaps after all, Mrs. Lawson was only softening up public opinion in favour of the drastic building exploit which her husband had in mind. For in 1878 the Georgian church was abandoned and a new edifice in the style of 1300 was designed by Arthur Blomfield. It has a fine spire which may be seen for miles round the countryside and whatever one may think of its size and suitability for a country congregation it is another of those churches which would grace a city suburb. Enjoying its third shelter is the effigy of a fourteenth-century cross-legged knight, probably one of the powerful local family of de Boteller and Eric Gill, the modern sculptor is responsible for memorials to the Martin family.

The present rectory by Sheward is a gracious house, one of the most handsome parsonages in the diocese. It was not always the rectory, but began life as Elmsleigh House in 1787 and was adopted to its sacred calling in 1895. It is the nearest thing the diocese possesses to an Adam house, with a delightful porch and fanlight and a good Georgian staircase, mouldings and fireplaces. It is hardly likely that it ever could be anything other than a parsonage since the new church must have been built on the front lawn of Elmsleigh House and the east window of the church is only a short distance from the front porch of the rectory.

In the vestry hangs a print of Dr. John Dee, one of the greatest scholars, mathematicians and astrologers of the age of Elizabeth I. He was given the benefice of Upton-on-Severn, no doubt as the custom then was, to finance his other more absorbing interests. Finally he became Warden of the Manchester Collegiate Church.

His was not a happy life and it is doubtful whether he ever came anywhere near Upton.

For the rest the visitor will derive much pleasure from strolling around this delightful town where life came to a pause when the Industrial Revolution struck the country. The Georgian houses on the waterside are evocative of the life of rich river merchants in a gracious age. There are charming half-timbered and Georgian houses in Church Street, the Anchor Inn dates from 1601 and it was probably the White Lion which Fielding had in mind when he related some of Tom Jones' adventures in Book 9 and chapter 3 onwards in his novel of that name.

A few more buildings in this neighbourhood must be noticed before we return to Worcester. Chief among these is Birtsmorton Court, surely the most perfect castle of a child's fairy romance. It seems to float on water as the swans lazily glide around its encircling moat. The architectural history of this very complicated series of buildings is hard to decipher. The north archway belongs to the fourteenth century, the parlour and adjacent room are probably attributable to Giles Nanfan about 1572 but Sir John Nanfan, 1446, and Sir Richard Nanfan, 1506, are also represented in the building. Wolsey must have moved in these two latters parts of the Court for he began his career here as secretary to Sir Richard, Lieutenant of Calais. William Huskisson, eminent politician and victim of the first railway accident in 1830 also lived here. But the Court could never have had a more colourful owner than the late Mr. Bradley Birt whom many of us knew as the indefatigable host who loved his home and enjoyed displaying it to his neighbours and friends when he entertained them on his birthday and at New Year when the boar's head was carried in with antique ceremonial.

The church is in the Decorated style with a Perpendicular west tower, but the eighteenth-century communion table of wrought iron with a marble top is a curiosity in a medieval church.

Ripple should by no means be missed. It is a large church for a small country village but its importance arose from its special association with the bishopric and it therefore rated as deserving a more elaborate church. There are parts of late twelfth to early thirteenth-century building but there is much rearrangement of earlier material in later alterations and rebuilding. To disentangle the architectural history would be a specialist task, but everyone can enjoy the 16 misericord stalls of the fifteenth century. The subjects, as at Malvern, are the labours of the months and there are also signs of the Zodiac. Ripple possessed a particularly fine Rectory of 1726 built by John Holt, who has a tablet in the church and who was of the same family who built Aston Hall in Birmingham. It was far too large and expensive for the modern parson and was sold in 1962 for £15,000. A very successful house in a neo-Georgian idiom by Peter Falconer and Co. replaced it.

A collection of small country churches must be noted as worth visiting. Castlemorton is Norman, but was much altered in repairs in the middle of the seventeenth century when it was reported as being very dilapidated. The astonishing heating apparatus should not and indeed could not be overlooked. Bannut Tree Farm, here, of 1890, is important as one of the earliest examples of C. F. A. Voysey's mature style. Longdon has a west tower of 1300, but is substantially Georgian of 1786. The Venetian window in the south aisle with its two large arched flanking windows is a pleasant classical variation. There is a good chandelier of 1789 and an elegant sarcophagus and obelisk by W. Stephens. Queenhill is associated with Longdon and has a Norman south doorway, a thirteenth-century chancel and a nice bit of early fourteenth-century armorial glass in the north window of the nave. By contrast, Pevsner says the east window, 1892, is ghastly. Eldersfield, again like so many of these churches, has remains from Norman times, probably 1160–1175, with late thirteenth-century chancel and early fourteenth-century north arcade: some good sixteenth-century benches with linenfold panels and a Jacobean pulpit. The stained glass includes seventeenth-century coats of arms. The surprisingly massive tower, crowned by a short spire, has carved niches on three of its sides. Berrow and Pendock are combined for ecclesiastical administration. The former has a Norman nave and chancel and a Norman font and there are later alterations in the Decorated and Perpendicular periods. The latter, built about 1170 has Norman decorative details, a Perpendicular west tower and some fifteenth-century linenfold panelling.

Finally, in this little rather remote south-west corner of the County is Bushley and here is something entirely different. The nineteenth century gets a chance to show its merits in a church by Blore, 1843 and a chancel by Scott, 1856. The march of ecclesiological taste is well illustrated in the work of the two architects. The earlier is working to Perpendicular models; but 13 years later the pundits have convinced the architects that Middle Pointed, 1300, is the only pure Gothic style. There is an imposing mansion here, too, built between 1836 and 1846 by Blore with Tudor and Jacobean memories in mind. It is now a school and the interior is treated with much richness.

So there is something for every architectural taste in this south-west corner, but visitors cannot fail to remark how prolific are the Norman remains as so often we find in these small country churches throughout Worcestershire.

We are very close to the Gloucester boundary here; cross the river by the bridge into Tewkesbury and you will be in our neighbour county. But we must turn our backs to the Severn and travel back to Worcester by another spoke of the wheel, marked on our maps as A38. Two further villages only merit our attention as we make speed for home. At Severn Stoke we are on the Croome Estate and its church of St. Denys again has Norman origins, but its big north tower, about 1300, has the picturesque feature of a stair turret rising above the roof of the tower itself. There are bits of ancient glass and tiles here. And the last village before Worcester is Kempsey, another Bishop's manor with a big church. It was big in 1200 but then enlarged further by a huge chancel of 1250 to 1260 with a fine east window of five lancet lights. There is also Decorated work of 1300 and some good fourteenth-century figures in stained glass in the chancel side windows. And if you have grown tired of architectural details you can look for the picture of the tree which grew to unusual proportions *inside* the church and which seems to have been a matter of pride to the worshippers rather than a distraction to their devotion.

There are many middling houses along this main road, both timber framed and Georgian and it is a pleasant game as you drive along to see if you can put a date to them. With the former it will not be easy as surviving half-timbered houses may have been built any time between 1300 and 1700. The wider the upright timbers the later the date, seems to be the only clue. With the Queen Anne and Georgian and Regency houses you will, if you have any interest in styles, be on firmer ground. There are plenty to choose from on this stretch of road. But soon they begin to be infilled or flanked by or even swallowed up in twentieth-century red brick and tiles. And then there is nothing but this red brick and pavements and street lighting because you are back at Worcester, home and dry.

CHAPTER FOUR

South-East towards the Cotswolds

Our next spoke lies to the south-east and takes us down to the south of the County, within sight of the Cotswold hills; the whole of this southern boundary of Worcestershire marches with Gloucestershire and the hills at Bredon and Broadway are out-fliers of the Cotswolds as their architecture betrays. There is a group of houses on the main road between Evesham and Broadway where it always seems to us the Cotswolds begin. For we pass sharply from the domain of half timber infilled with plaster or brick and from brick cottages to this group which are built of the pure honey-coloured stone of the Cotswolds; and immediately we are in the territory of stone houses with pointed gables and stone mullions and ball finials and casement windows. So the much imitated Cotswold architecture has begun. In this south-east section of the County we find dozens of small villages, hamlets and churches which in this chapter can only rate at a line or two each and may even be omitted, for we may remember that Domesday Book mentioned 60 priests in 57 places, and this is the region where we shall find their churches even though they may not have been mentioned in the Book, for here the bulk of the medieval population of Worcestershire was sited.

Two roads lead away from the city to the south. Both are reached by leaving the Cathedral hub and travelling along Sidbury. Soon the Bath Road branches off to the right and leads us on through Kempsey and Severn Stoke to Tewkesbury. But our route continues into the London Road beyond and takes its right turn at a roundabout a little beyond Ebenezer Baylis' Printing works, a great press where Churchill's memoirs, among many other notable modern books,

were printed; another distinction for Worcester craftsmanship. Also in this area is the vast new Girls' Grammar School and, a little further along the road where we have turned, the famous Worcester College for the Blind, first established at the Commandery in 1866 but moved to its present site in 1902. It is rich in equipment and all the modern devices for the teaching of the blind, so that its scholars receive a Grammar School education which often leads them on to Universities and high places in their chosen professions.

Now we are set on the Whittington Road which leads to some of the most famous of our Worcestershire names, to Pershore, to Evesham, to Bredon and to Broadway. Soon, on our left is Whittington Church by A. E. Perkins who began the great Cathedral restoration; it dates from 1842 and its principal feature is its unusually thin stone bell turret. On the other side of the main road is a place whose name was well known to recruits in two world wars, Norton Barracks, built in 1876; the recent disappearance of the Worcestershire Regiment as a separate Army Unit may wring some nostalgia even from the tough heart of many a soldier trained there. The Norman foundation of the parish church here is largely obscured by the Victorian restorations. But Norman fragments remain and the tower comes from the Perpendicular period. Along this main road too, on the left-hand side before we reach Pershore are two more churches, one of medieval foundation, Stoulton and Drakes Broughton. The first has a Norman nave and chancel of about 1130 with a tower rebuilt in 1936; there is a good Norman font and a helmet and a short sword said to be of Italian workmanship of about 1470. The second church is entirely Victorian, built by W. J. Hopkins in 1857.

Between the Bath Road and the London Road is the Croome Estate and since we are not very rich in stately houses in Worcestershire, it would be profitable to linger for a while at Croome Court, which is one of our finest. This was the seat of the Coventry family but is now occupied by the Society of St. Vincent de Paul, who conduct here a school for sub-normal children. The Coventry family have given great service to the nation; the first Lord Coventry was Lord Keeper of England and we shall find his monument with the Great Seal in the church. His descendants followed in public service and it was the sixth Earl who created the house we see today.

18 (opposite) Pershore Abbey – lantern tower

Happily the family are still with us but a series of deaths, with their accompanying voracious death duties led to retrenchment and the abandonment of this great house. The present Earl lives appropriately at Earl's Croome and we may be grateful that this beneficent Roman Catholic order found a use for the Court and rescued it from the dereliction into which, like Strensham, it might so easily have fallen.

Croome Court was begun in 1751. Its architect was Lancelot Brown, which is at least surprising since that is a name which we usually associate with landscape gardening. He was no doubt helped by Sanderson Miller of Radway and certainly we see the hand of Kent and Robert Adam in the building. Here is a monument to the strict Palladian style as mediated to this country by Inigo Jones. Those low square angle eminences with pyramidal roofs are a clear reminiscence of Wilton and we shall see them again at Hagley, a house which has similarities to Croome. There is a splendid entrance on either side of the house, the main entrance with a spacious two-armed open staircase and the other, or garden entrance, with a tetra-style portico of unfluted Doric columns.

Inside, though necessarily overlaid with the educational flotsam of a special school it is surprising how much of the original classical decoration still survives. One room was removed entirely to the Metropolitan Museum in New York, but its features have been replaced by facsimiles; it formerly contained a set of Boucher Neilson Gobelins tapestries. The entrance hall, with its four Doric columns and the Saloon, with a sumptuous pedimented back doorway, show the style of Kent. Surprisingly the Saloon still retains several of the family portraits, including one of Maria Gunning, one of the three celebrated beautiful Gunning sisters for whom the sixth Earl probably built the house. She did not live long to enjoy it; only nine years. She died as a result of clogged pores from too much make-up. The library in the south east corner of the house introduces us to the delicate plaster work of Robert Adam, executed between 1761 and 1763. But his chief work is the long gallery, with its white sculptured caryatids holding a garland and its six alcoves filled with figures from the antique, and panelled sketches in grisaille. The ceiling with its sunk octagon panels and incised mouldings, all work of the early 1760s, is supposed to be based on the Villa Madama at Rome.

The garden buildings, alas, seem to be in a state of irreclaimable dereliction. They were among the finest of Adam's achievements in this line. The principal entrance gateway fortunately survives, based on the gateway at Palmyra and reminiscent of Adam's work at Harewood. The gardens must have been quite spectacular in the nineteenth century. A fascinating book entitled *Hortus Croomensis and Observations on the Propagation of Exotics*, published in 1824 by William Dean who describes himself as 'Botanic Gardener to the Rt. Hon. the Earl of Coventry', lists scores of rare plants which were grown in the gardens at that time. It is a slight book but has a certain usefulness in indicating what the house looked like and how the pictures were disposed at that time. He quotes a writer in the *Gentleman's Magazine* in 1792, who concluded his glowing encomium on the house and gardens by saying: 'If there be any spot on the habitable globe to make a death bed terrible, it is Lord Coventry's at Croome.'

Nevertheless their Lordships did their best to make even that aweful dissolution tolerable, for the parish church rebuilt on a nearby hill provides a handsome mausoleum which must have been some compensation for quitting the glories of Croome. It is an 'eye catcher' and yet a surprisingly effective bit of Gothic experimentation in an unlikely period. Marcus Whiffen declares that it is the result of a collaboration between Sanderson Miller and Robert Adam, commissioned in 1761. Pevsner, on the other hand, believes, in his pleasing phrase that 'Capability' Brown was responsible for the 'carcase' and Adam for the interior and furnishings. The tower is a particularly satisfactory piece of work and might deceive the unwary into a close comparison with Somerset towers of the fifteenth century. 'Daintiness' and 'prettiness' are epithets used of the furnishings, but essentially, of course, the church is a mausoleum and the great array of funeral monuments in the chancel is a symposium of Coventry family records from 1639 removed from a previous building.

Croome Church is, we would venture to say, one of the most important churches in the 'Strawberry Hill Gothick' idiom, not only in Worcestershire but also in the whole country. Unfortunately it has no congregation and little support, for the day has long passed when an estate church such as this could be crammed with the serried ranks of family guests and servants of the Great House. There is a representative problem here. Some churches can be consigned—as Croome has in fact been consigned—to the care of the Redundant Churches fund which has at present adequate means to keep the building repaired and watertight and to provide the services of a caretaker. There is much to be thankful for in this evidence of generosity shared by the State and the Church Commissioners. But it is doubtful whether this can ever be a final solution to an intractable problem. It is extremely difficult to discover any adequate alternative use for such a redundant church in the isolated country; the problem may be easier in an urban area where such buildings may be wanted and useful alternate employment found. But what is to be done in the deep country to ensure such buildings against further depredation and vandalism? A solution tarries.

Pirton church, also on the Croome Estate, not far away, is a treasure of a different kind. The half-timbered tower is of very early date, perhaps even earlier than the fourteenth century; there is a Norman nave and a Decorated chancel. The Pirton Stone, $4\frac{3}{4}''$ by $3\frac{1}{2}''$ has always been an object of much antiquarian speculation. It bears a carved Crucifixion and also the figure of a bishop and the model of a church. The latest suggestion is that it was a die for the casting of pilgrims' badges, that the church represents Canterbury Cathedral and that the whole thing may be as early as the eleventh century. It is one of the most precious antiquarian relics in the County.

In palmier days, the heir of the Earl of Coventry lived at Pirton Court with the title of Viscount Deerhurst. This is a large sixteenth-century half-timbered house, very much restored. Pirton Rectory, a big square Queen Anne house, was sold out of the uses of the church a few years ago.

We now return to the London Road and travel to Pershore, one of our most delightful Worcestershire Georgian towns. Everyone has heard of Pershore even if only in connection with Pershore plums, and this town is in fact the headquarters of a very flourishing fruit-growing industry, set on the Avon and surrounded with rich orchards which produce all types of fruit. As a town only it would be a joy to visit and to stroll about its Georgian streets, but at the heart of it is a building which in its entirety must have been glorious indeed and which even now, as only a fragment of its former self, is a gem in the crown of our English Gothic heritage. In Pershore Abbey we have so much less than has been preserved for us, wondrously, at Worcester and Malvern, yet, thankfully, so much more than at Evesham where destruction was very nearly total. The visitor to Pershore for the first time will be struck with the two great modern buttresses of 1913; and they are there of course because the great tower must be secured and the sturdy nave, which would have done that, has disappeared except for its two eastern-most Norman piers. All that we have left in this strangely truncated building is this bit of nave, the crossing, over which soars the majestic tower, the transepts, the chancel and the modern apse.

A wide expanse of green sward leads to the west door between the modern buttresses. Can we imagine a great Norman nave, like Tewkesbury or Gloucester, stretching westwards; for the intact Pershore Abbey was 325 ft. long, exactly the same length as Tewkesbury and a little shorter than the original Norman Cathedral of Gloucester which was 365 ft. Only a situation such as this and a comparison with surviving buildings can really impress us with the vast destruction which was wrought at the Dissolution.

The Abbey, which bears the name of Holy Cross, appears to have been founded as a community of secular canons as early as 690. There were various alterations of status until it became a regular establishment of Benedictine monks who received their charter from King Edgar in 972, a year which provided recently for a wonderfully organised and highly comprehensive millennium celebration. It was richly endowed with lands in Worcestershire and Gloucestershire and with salt pans at Droitwich, but it lost heavily in its resources when King Edward alienated large portions of its land to enrich his new foundation at Westminster. The close connection between Pershore and Westminster is exemplified by the fact that the Dean and Chapter of Westminster are still patrons of the living of Pershore. The Abbey was dissolved in 1539 and no sign of the conventual buildings remains.

The earliest traces of building are some pieces of walling in the transept, which are of mid-eleventh-century date, and there is other walling in the transept together with the piers and arches of the crossing which date from about 1100. This was probably the date of the Norman nave which would have borne comparison with the naves of Tewkesbury and Gloucester. The arches of the crossing are very high, about 50 ft. There is evidence of fires from time to time which called forth new building experimentation, and so we get a rebuilding of 1239 which gives us the glorious structure of the choir which we see today; yet another fire gave opportunity for the presbytery to be vaulted about 1330 and the tower above the crossing to be rebuilt. This tower is of singularly beautiful design incorporating details which are reminiscent of Salisbury, with much ball-flower ornament, characteristic of the period; its lower stage is really a lantern of great beauty. The cunning arrangement of flying buttresses which take the thrust of the chancel vault should be noted, and the extremely beautiful and almost geometrically patterned lierne and tierceron vaulting with its intricate pattern and its large naturalistically carved bosses. The arches of the arcading, a wall passage and the unusually high clerestory lancets build up into a lovely architectural composition which has little to rival it in this country. Only the chancel apse is modern, 1847; there was a restoration by Scott in 1862 and a further one by Sir Harold Brakspear early in this century.

Among the furnishings are a twelfth-century font, a cross-legged knight of 1280 and the tomb of a fourteenth-century abbot. Family monumental reminiscences include the tomb of Fulk and Dorothea Haselwood of 1569; the effigies of the parents have gone but ten children remain, three sons, six daughters and an infant. But that is not the end of the Haselwood family, for in the south transept is a table tomb under a tester of a man in early seventeenth-century armour, and this is probably Thomas, the son of Fulk.

St. Andrew, the other church in the town, was first built in the eleventh century, but what we see now is some late twelfth-century work in the north aisle and the rest mostly early fifteenth-century work. This building, which was not required as a place of worship and which, when Prof. Pevsner wrote his account, was reported as being in a very bad state has since, happily, been the subject of very considerable expenditure which has restored it to a life of new usefulness as a Parish Centre. This is a conspicuous example of the proper use of a redundant church to which we have made reference. For £14,000, towards which the restorers were helped by a gift from the Pilgrim Trust, the town has been enriched with another public building of which it should be proud.

A stroll around the town makes another of those Georgian perambulations for which we have several opportunities in Worcestershire. Here we may begin at the Avon bridge which still incorporates some medieval parts and walk back up Bridge Street, where the two façades of smaller Georgian houses are sufficiently unaltered to retain their original charm and dignity. Nearer the centre of the town some of the houses are on quite the grand scale. Perrott House, now an antique shop, was built in 1760 and is rich in interior detail. There is a handsome staircase and delicate stucco work which seems pretty good evidence that Judge Perrott who built the house must have employed the services of the craftsmen who were working in the Adam idiom at the nearby Croome Court. Barclay's Bank, of the late eighteenth century with its elaborate doorway and fanlight, is also impressive and across the road is the Three Tuns Hotel whose intricate Regency ironwork is a reminder that the similar charms of Cheltenham artistry are not many miles ahead. The Angel Hotel is in yet another style; its front was rebuilt in 1920 but there are sixteenth-century fixtures inside. And there are many other houses and buildings to be picked out in every style from half-timbered to the Victorian. Pershore is a rewarding experience for the enthusiast in townscape and domestic architecture.

Two different routes lead away from Pershore. We may follow the main London Road to Evesham or pass through Broad Street, which is so broad that it is really a Market Square, and, taking the road to the left at the bottom, pass through Council building property beyond the warehouses, which bespeak the fruit-growing prosperity of the town, and then turn left opposite the cemetery entrance on to the Bredon road. There is a road running off this exit from the town which bears the intriguing title 'NO GAINS'. Enquiry from a native elicited the information that 'Granny used to say' that in far away times the site of these houses was allotments which proved to be so disastrously unproductive that the land attracted this somewhat sinister title which was afterwards commemorated in the name of the road.

Besford to the east of Pershore is of some importance because of its big house and its church. The former, Besford Court, now insti-tutionalised and run by the Society of St. Vincent de Paul in associa-tion with Croome Court, is a fine timbered house of about 1500 with notable extensions by an important modern architect, Randall Wells. Wells was connected with Lethaby, who built the famous 'Arts and Crafts' church of Brockhampton in Herefordshire, and the front of Besford Court in the Tudor style displays some of the skills inherent in the building of that notable church. The interior with its two staircases and the cloister and the gallery are particularly exciting. But the old church at Besford is equally noteworthy for it is the only timber-framed church in the County, dating in its earliest parts from the mid-fourteenth century. The complete rood loft parapet is a treasure and the monuments to the Harewell family, one a painted triptych with movable wings, are unusually fascinating. The triptych is probably by the same hand as its more famous counterpart at Burford in Shropshire, signed by Michael Salabos, 1588.

The road from Pershore to Bredon passes through two parishes. Birlingham has a Perpendicular west tower but the rest of the church was rebuilt in 1872 by Benjamin Ferrey, distinguished Victorian church architect and friend and biographer of Augustus W. Pugin. It was a curious idea to remove the Norman chancel arch from the old church and use it for the churchyard entrance; but at any rate it preserved it. Worcestershire people are probably more interested in the wide-spreading carpeting of the churchyard with snowdrops and crocuses and other spring flowers; they come in large numbers to see this unusually prolific display each year. The old parsonage of 1774 has long been abandoned in favour of more convenient accom-modation, but we came across the original architect's plans for this house in the County Record Office some years ago. The road con-tinues through low-lying meadowland over which the Avon frequently floods; the bridge which carries this busy main road into the village of Eckington is still the medieval bridge, narrow, hump-backed and something of a traffic hazard and Eckington, which is largely a village strung out along the road, has difficult traffic and parking problems. The west end of its Norman church comes very close to the road in the centre of the village; it is an unusually wide church with two aisles, the south arcade made up of round, very late Norman piers, the north aisle and arcade dating from the last century. The south-west tower is Perpendicular and the chancel is fourteenth century. There is a good Jacobean monument here to John Hanford in the style of the famous sculptor Epiphanius Evesham.

The spire of Bredon church beckons us on and this, at the start, is hopeful, for spires are very unusual in Worcestershire. We are not to be disappointed, for this great finger which dominates the countryside indicates one of the best-known names in the County and one of its finest churches. No doubt Bredon, to most strangers, signifies the famous hill, but as a matter of fact the hill is some considerable distance from the village and if you started here with the intention of climbing, you would have a good tramp before you reached the foot. So perhaps we had better begin with the attractions of the village and they, of course, begin at the church. It is large by village standards with architecture of every period exemplified in the structure. You may like best the great Norman west front reminiscent of Tewkesbury, capped by two Norman pinnacles, or the Norman nave; or you may prefer the very lovely south chapel, a gem of Early English work of about 1250. The chancel is later than this, perhaps about 1300, and the north arcade is Perpendicular. In fact all our native architectural styles from the Conquest to the Reformation are represented here.

But the church is a treasure house not only because of its architectural framework but also because of what it contains. The stained glass in the north chancel window with its two female saints is early fourteenth century and very fine. There is red trellised wall painting in the chancel and a wide selection of fourteenth-century heraldic tiles. The stone monuments are outstanding; an Easter Sepulchre in the chancel and a fine coffin lid with a cross somewhat mutilated but with male and female effigies above the arms; then a late medieval tomb recess with husband and wife and child. Strangest of all, perhaps, is a carved shield with a pair of outreaching hands, holding a heart, no doubt a memorial to a heart burial at this spot. Then in the south or Mytton chapel is the superb Reed monument of 1611, to Giles, armoured, and Katherine his wife, richly apparelled in the costume of the period and their four children. A modern tablet, near by, inscribed in good contemporary lettering, records the exemplary restoration of this most important Jacobean monument by the Cottrell family.

Bredon was a Bishop's manor before the end of the 8th century and there was a monastic settlement here. Not in pomp and glory, however, did Bishop Prideaux find sanctuary when he was dispossessed of the Worcester bishopric in the Civil War. He subsisted and died in deep poverty and his gravestone of 1650 is on the chancel floor. However, there are substantial houses here and not least the Rectory where Bishop Prideaux found refuge with his son-in-law, Dr. Henry Sutton. This was, until recent years, an enormous house matching what passed until times of inflation as an opulently endowed benefice. It was in the patronage of the Duke of Portland, who sometimes presented one of his relatives to the living. Lady Ottoline Morrell describes how she stayed at this house in the reign of her relative, the Revd. H. G. Cavendish Browne, with 15 servants and fires lit in 18 rooms daily. This was not the life-style of the average mid-twentieth-century clergyman, and in the 1950s a most skilful restoration and rearrangement was carried out by Mr. Maurice Jones which created three living units from the existing building. The largest portion, which forms the present rectory, is still over-large to suit most clerical tastes and its future as a rectory is still in the balance. It is an important house, though it has lost its original configuration by much division and alteration; there is a splendid timbered roof which indicates that it may date as far back as the fifteenth or sixteenth century, but certainly many changes were made in Elizabethan times when it is possible that the great hall was divided both vertically and horizontally.

The old Mansion is a fine seventeenth-century brick house with dormers and mullions and the Manor House is a five-bayed stone house of the eighteenth century with rather poor classical details. There is Hancock's School, anciently endowed by one of the owners of Bredon's Norton Manor and there are the Reed Almshouses of 1696. But most important is the splendid Tithe Barn, one of the finest in existence, dating from the thirteenth or early fourteenth century. It measures 124 ft. and has aisles and two porches one of which contains an upper room with a fireplace. This splendid building is now in the care of the National Trust.

The Fox and Hounds, a timber-framed hostelry, is a welcoming port of call for those who essay a climb of the hill or who, having done that, feel themselves entitled to some refreshment. It is also a place where there is much talk about yachts and cabin cruisers for sailing has developed greatly in recent years, and Bredon is finding a new road to prosperity in the leasing of moorings on the Avon banks. A few years ago in the bar here it would have been possible to enjoy the racy conversation of Mr. John Moore, whose early death was a sad deprivation in the field of English letters. Somehow or other, Worcestershire has never been prolific in regional novelists, but in his chronicles of Brensham and the thinly veiled country and town near here, Worcestershire, and Gloucestershire, had a distinguished practitioner in that particular literary *genre*. His expertise as well as his appreciation of human relationships seemed to improve with each novel. Had not death removed him prematurely from the literary scene it is more than likely that he would have been writing very great novels indeed.

But Bredon Hill dominates all this scene and is a comparatively easy climb for reasonably active people. Its best ascents are from Bredon's Norton, Westmancote, Kemerton or Elmley Castle. Its height is 360 ft. and the views from the summit on a clear day are spectacular in every direction. Lovers of *Tom Jones* will recollect their hero's ascent with Partridge when 'Mazard Hill' presented them with a view which seemed to them one of the noblest prospects in the world; and, at a later date, A. E. Housman, a Worcestershire man of letters whom we shall meet again at Bromsgrove, allowed his poetic fancy to present an idyll of a Sunday morning which began with 'coloured counties' seen from the summit, and the sound of larks, but which progressed to a tragic end. But tragic events of a substantial sort had, in truth, occurred on Bredon's summit. An ancient fort there belongs to the second century B.C.; but early in the first century A.D. the fort which may have been continuously occupied from its earliest time came to a violent end. Fifty bodies of defenders were excavated there, victims of tribal expansion of a new people from the south-east.

Bredon Hill is ringed around with a string of pretty villages which contain churches and houses which all deserve inspection. Perhaps we had better begin with Overbury, where everything is on a grand scale and in exquisite tidiness as befits the headquarters of the Holland-Martin clan with its family fortunes based on the venerable Martin's Bank. Overbury Court is an early eighteenth-century stone house with gardens beautifully maintained; it has been modernised and improved constantly over the years and there is a little evidence of Norman Shaw's work of 1895 and the recent work of Victor Heal in 1959. Norman Shaw is also represented in the village hall of 1895 and every age and style finds a place in its tidy groups of cottages. The red brick Victorian Gothic vicarage of the usual run-of-the-mill pattern is a bit of a disappointment and an anachronism. But there is nothing disappointing about the impeccably maintained churchyard and church. There is a Norman nave and a dominating Perpendicular central tower, but the Early English chancel with its rib vaulting and bosses is an unusually enriching feature in a moderate-sized village church; a church altogether congruous with its opulent setting.

Round the hill to the west is Bredon's Norton with its long nave of the early thirteenth century and its Norman south doorway. Much of this church is reputed to have been rebuilt after a fire, but the late seventeenth century memorial to William Hancock and his wife, the founder of the free school in Bredon, is well preserved in the chancel. Further up the hill are two important houses, one, Norton Park built in the Tudor style at the surprisingly early date of 1830 and the other, the Elizabethan manor, built by Thomas Copley, whose arms together with its date 1585 appear on the building. It has a fine great hall and an 18 ft. dining table which has been there since Copley built the house. Norton Park became the home of a very remarkable woman, Mrs. Woodhull-Martin, when she married John Biddulph Martin, a scion of the Overbury family, in 1883. A remarkable woman indeed; the only woman who has contended for the Presidency of the United States of America. In her younger days she was a savage polemic for 'Women's Lib.' in every facet of female activity. One account of her, among several recently written, describes her as 'The free lover who ran for President'. But married to John B. Martin and permanently domiciled in England she became in truth a reformed character. When she was able to get the old Manor House into her hands at the beginning of the century she restored it and established it first as a Ladies' Agricultural College and then as a centre for Anglo-American friendship.

She was a great propagandist and *littérateuse*; indeed at one period she had published her own newspaper in the States. Pageants of various kinds were a favourite form of entertainment staged by her at Bredon's Norton Manor and in its great barn which she equipped as a village hall. One of these held in 1920 had very singular consequences. In one episode, written by her, great play was made of a visit of Sir Walter Raleigh to Thomas Copley at the manor when the owner was to sail as a colleague of Raleigh to the new world. In 1924 this incident was solemnly taken up and incorporated by Dr. J. F. Muirhead in his *American Shrines in English Soil*; since then almost every writer on this neighbourhood and every guide book has eagerly transmitted the story of Thomas Copley as a colonising adventurer with Raleigh in Virginia. How Victoria Woodhull-Martin would have laughed! Exhaustive research has failed to reveal the slightest connection between Copley and Raleigh. The whole Raleigh legend was cooked up in her fertile brain to give romantic colour to her pageant. But thus history is made!

The next manor house round the hill is Woollas Hall, a rather grander version of Bredon's Norton Manor which it resembles in some details, built in 1611. It is a gabled house and contains within a screen with Ionic pilasters and an elaborate chimney-piece and over-mantel. But this house has been a good deal mutilated and spoilt since it was cut up into flats.

Elmley Castle is a beautiful village. Robert le Despencer's castle, which gave it its name, has long since disappeared and the great house of the Davies family which succeeded it has likewise been demolished, but its delightful church with its imposing array of monuments, some of the best in the County, still remains. The main street, tree lined and with picturesque rows of houses leads up to the fifteenth-century village cross and then to the fifteenth-century embattled church. There has been much rebuilding here, perhaps from Saxon times, and the chancel dates from before 1100; then there is a thirteenth-century tower and some fourteenth-century arches and the fifteenth-century battlements which create the main impression. But the Savage memorials which, in truth, some-what overcrowd the church are the things to examine here. The table tomb of William Savage, who died in 1616, and his son Giles, who died in 1631, with Giles's wife Katherine and their children is one of the finest things of its kind in existence. Mrs. Esdaile in her classic book, *English Church Monuments*, compares this sculpture to the tomb of Mrs. Arthur Coke at Bramfield, Suffolk, allowing that both may be from the studio of Nicholas Stone and speaking of them as two of the great works of art of England. Then there is the monument of Thomas, Lord Coventry, who died in 1699; this should, by rights, have been in Croome church, but his son refused it entry and it found its way to Elmley Castle because Thomas's widow had married, secondly, William Savage. It was said that the second Lord Coventry had no love for the lady who was, in any case, his step-mother.

A little to the north of Elmley Castle but still within the shadow of the hill lie the Combertons, Great and Little. The former has a Perpendicular tower probably built on the foundation of a Norman nave, some stalls with Jacobean panels and some sixteenth-century benches with plain ends; the latter, again a Perpendicular tower, three Norman windows in the nave, moved from elsewhere, and a rather crude tympanum. It also has some bits of old glass in the south-west window and some fifteenth-century tiles in the chancel. Finally, to conclude these hill villages, on the south side on the Gloucester border and both churches in fact in the Gloucester diocese are Kemerton and Beckford. Kemerton, by Richard C. Carpenter, 1845, rates at a reproduced print in Goodhart-Rendel's *English Architecture since the Regency*. The print calls it St. Alban's, its supporters today St. Nicholas'; someone has blundered. The print's caption is 'The Tractarian Paragon' and it remains today much as it was built, the ecclesiologist's dream. The style is largely fourteenth century and there still hangs the massive corona by Hardman which looks as though it might have come out of the medieval court in the 1851 exhibition. It hangs in the contemporary print and it is good to know that such examples of ornate Victorian craftsmanship are better valued today. Forty years ago we were throwing them out; we know better now.

Beckford takes us back to the genuine medieval article, Norman, with some reminiscences of Malvern Priory. There is a tympanum and much good Norman decoration here with a suggestion of the Herefordshire school of carvers. The tympanum has the Harrowing of Hell and there are beasts' heads, a human head and a centaur; altogether, a rewarding church for those who like Norman detail. Beckford Hall is Jacobean, but as befits a house which stands on the site of an 1128 priory of Augustinian canons, it now houses a branch of the Roman Catholic Salesian order.

Having now traversed Bredon Hill and its encircling villages we can take the main Tewkesbury–Evesham road and travel north-east to Evesham. On the route is Ashton-under-Hill with a thirteenth-century tower and a Gothic chancel of 1624, which demonstrates again that the older tradition of building was not quite extinguished by the Renaissance though, as here, the stream was flowing very thinly. Sedgeberrow dates from 1331 but has an additional interest from having been restored by Butterfield in 1866. The Victorianisation goes a little too far for most people, but the church is tall and dignified and the windows, reredos and screen, all by Butterfield, have a certain validity in their own right. Hinton-on-the-Green is our last call before Evesham. There is a Norman nave, a doorway with a tympanum and a late Victorian chancel, 1895. The architect this time is Sedding. A late fifteenth-century incised slab to a priest is the principal monument here. This benefice has lately been united with Sedgeberrow and the Victorian vicarage awaits demolition. The Laslett's trustees whose almshouses we have encountered in Friar Street, Worcester, own much land in this parish as well as the patronage of the living.

So we arrive at Evesham, which is another of our great Worcestershire names, a place of immemorial fertility in its market gardening and still adhering to its unusual 'customs' in matters of land tenure. Evesham 'growers' are men of hard work and endless inventiveness in their methods of devising heavier crops; their 'canniness', which is proverbial, arises from the great risks they are always under when unpropitious weather is easily capable of wiping out in a night a whole season's labour and profit. But to most visitors Evesham is a matter of a ruined abbey and Simon de Montfort. There is a close connection between the two for the body of the great constitutionalist soldier was horribly mutilated and his trunk buried before the high altar of the Abbey Church. It became a place of pilgrimage and a spring at a spot where he fell was supposed to have the curative properties of the *locus sanctus* of a martyr. But what remains of the splendid abbey now? Only a bit of the north transept of the church, the entrance arch of the Chapter House with its twin niches, and, supremely, the glorious campanile of Abbot Lichfield's tower.

The Abbey was founded in 714 by Bishop Egwin of Worcester. There were rebuildings after the Conquest in the eleventh and twelfth and thirteenth centuries and the bell tower comes from the early sixteenth century, shortly before the Reformation. The splendours of the Abbey in its prime were said to include 16 altars, 164 gilded pillars and the shrines and relics of Saxon saints and the tomb of Simon de Montfort. It was vast in extent, covering the greensward on which children now play, but all there is for the visitor to see today is the fragments mentioned and the great tower, built by an enterprising abbot who so little read the signs of the times that he could have had no notion of the all-consuming disaster which was shortly to burst upon his own handiwork and upon scores of similar monastic buildings, elsewhere

Near by in the town is the Cemetery Gate, which connected the abbey cemetery with the town, and next to it the old vicarage which the present vicar uses as his office. This seems to be a fifteenth-century house with some traces of painted decoration. The remains of the Great Gate, part of the building of Abbot Cheriton in the fourteenth century are incorporated into a Georgian house of 1711 and further west, delightfully preserved, is a timber-framed house of the fourteenth or fifteenth century, now known as the Almonry and housing a useful local museum.

The curiosity to many visitors is the proximity of two churches, All Saints and St. Lawrence in the same churchyard. One may have been a cemetery church and the other the parish church. They present an almost insuperable problem for parochial administration in these days. All Saints looks like Perpendicular work but certainly

19 (*opposite above*) Bredon – *Great Tithe Barn*
20 (*below*) Broadway – 'England's loveliest village'

derives originally from the Norman period; its gem is the Lichfield Chapel with its fan vaulting built by Abbot Lichfield for his own burial about 1513. St. Lawrence was heavily restored by Eginton in 1836; it is mostly Perpendicular work but has a north aisle entirely by Eginton. In the south chapel again there is magnificent fan vaulting and elaborate niches flanking the east window.

The two traffic arteries in the town are Bridge Street and High Street generally heavily congested, especially at holiday seasons. For Evesham has certainly laid itself out to attract visitors who flock from all directions towards this historic name. Although in fact the town has less to offer of ecclesiastical architectural treasure than Worcester or Malvern or Pershore, it must be said that its enterprise in the splendid laying out of the Avon banks and the riverside meadows makes it a most rewarding destination for family picnics. Nor need the antiquarian minded or the architectural enthusiast be disappointed in his stroll around these two main streets. They abound with fine specimens from every period. Perhaps the skilfully restored Booth Hall, a late fifteenth-century house in the middle of the town, is the most outstanding, but there are many others which should not be missed; through the Norman gate on the left, the Bedehouses of Abbot Zattoni; in the Market Place, the neo-Georgian library of 1908; the houses and Crown Hotel in Bridge Street and a whole series of Caroline and Georgian houses in High Street. There is a symposium of every sort of style in this market town which, above all, gives one the impression of being intensely alive. Growing up, no doubt, around the prosperity of an Abbey that was a great centre of pilgrimage, Evesham has survived the total disaster of what was its chiefest treasure, and the rich alluvial soil has perpetuated its natural function of supplying its delicious vegetable produce whilst monks come and monks go, into a commercial and computerised age which in spite of its monstrous cleverness cannot survive without these natural fruits of the earth.

Broadway is the end of our present spoke and it is not far from Evesham to Broadway. The route lies down Bridge Street and across the second and older Evesham bridge (Worcester still has only one) when we find ourselves in the ancient parish of Bengeworth which is now really Evesham-over-the-river. Bengeworth's old church has

21 (*opposite above*) *Evesham – Two Churches and Abbey Tower*
22 (*below*) *Evesham Abbey – The Almonry*

disappeared except for the lowest stage of a south tower and a grave-yard, but its new church, 1870, by T. D. Barry of Liverpool, stands by a roundabout further along the main road. It has a tall spire and an arcade of granite columns. The 1709 monument to John Deacle removed from the old church to the south transept here and the sixteenth-century tablet to Thomas Watson are the principal things to look for. Deacle was a prosperous merchant who was not unmindful of his native place and educational charity still benefits from his bequests. He is portrayed as half rising from the ground; not in the full confidence of the carefree posture of Lord Foley at Great Witley, but sufficiently assured not to be lying entirely prostrate. A charming little portrait in stained glass in one of the south aisle windows com-memorates a local craftsman who gave much of his time and skill in adorning his beloved church and is a gracious reminder that the meek are sometimes blessed and not always forgotten. The Victorian vicarage here has been entirely demolished since Pevsner commended it in 1968.

Wickhamford lies to the left of the main road as we press on, a medieval church with a seventeenth-century west tower. The great thing here is the splendid double monument to Sir Samuel and Sir Edward Sandys, father and son and their wives and children. Some of its details show Gothic survivals in a Jacobean composition. Mrs. Esdaile, in high praise, puts this monument in a group which she designates as the finest in the country by one hand, though the hand is unspecified. The sixteenth-century manor house near the church is timber framed and much restored. Those who wish to know more about the personal associations of this church and the house where he grew up may find information in the somewhat skittish novel autobiography of James Lees-Milne.

So we arrive at Broadway, at the end of the spoke, and Fish Hill and Snowshill Manor and Chipping Campden and all the delights of the Cotswolds lie only a little ahead. But these are in Gloucester-shire. It is no use being superior about Broadway and talking in disparaging terms about commercialisation and sophistication. If people want to come and look at this lovely place they must be housed and fed and they have every right to buy some reminiscence of their visit. For, by every criterion, Broadway is a very lovely place indeed and fully deserves its world-wide reputation. Its main street is immensely long and wide, its buildings are the very acme of Cotswold architecture, from the large and celebrated Lygon Arms to the smaller cottages which line the route. Well has it been called 'the show village of England'; its beauty has attracted many distinguished residents throughout the years, its property is fabulously expensive and it is reputed to be much favoured in these days by film stars and similar opulently placed persons who can afford its prices.

The modern church in the village by Eginton, 1839, is perhaps a little disappointing in such a setting, but St. Eadburga's, which lies some distance away on the Snowshill road, is the real parish church, originating about 1200 but externally mostly Perpendicular. There are many antiquarian treasures among the furnishings, font, pulpit, screen, benches and so on. It would be a pity to miss this important church because it is not obviously in the village; services are still held there in the lighter days of summer time.

Broadway has attained yet another mead of fame in recent years as the home of some of the most inspired modern craftsmanship. The products in wood of Gordon Russell, whose modern factory demonstrates that industry need not necessarily do violence to the most exquisite of natural environments, have been sufficiently publicised by all the media as to establish a national reputation. Truly, Broadway deserves all that has been written and said about it in highest praise. And if we dislike crowds we can always visit it in the off-season periods when they are no longer there to obstruct our view of all these lovely village façades.

The town of Evesham is ringed with a score of villages with their churches and houses which we have no space to describe in detail. Perhaps it would be most useful to pick out a few of the significant things which should not be missed, but visitors will discover many more for themselves if they take the trouble to explore the vale with its territory as rich in antiquarian lore as its fields are rich in market produce. There is Norton with its splendid Bigg monuments, Elizabethan and Jacobean; again stylistically related to Epiphanius Evesham and the Hanford monument at Eckington. Even more important here is the stone lectern with its seated figure of a cleric and richly carved foliage; it is generally accepted as having come

from Evesham Abbey and, if so, its late twelfth-century craftsmanship assigns it to the reign of Abbot Adam. The Lenches are a cluster
of charming and remote little villages; the most significant is the
church at Rous Lench which was dramatically restored and re-
furbished by Mr. Chafy, the rich squarson, in the last century. He
found many treasures there and added more. It is a Norman church
and supreme, over the south doorway, is the seated Christ in an
almond-shaped glory of mid-twelfth-century date. One wonders
whether Mr. Graham Sutherland might have found some inspiration
for his great East wall tapestry at Coventry in this or some similar
figure. To the squarson we owe Preedy's north chapel, the north
aisle apse, the screen and the Italianate baldacchino. There are other
preserved fragments and monuments from every age. It is all very
surprising in a remote country church. Rous Lench Court, where the
Reverend Mr. Chafy lived, is an imposing half-timbered mansion, but
a good deal of it is reproduction in early Victorian times; the terraced
gardens and sculpture are spectacular. But there is not much left of
the house where Richard Baxter is said to have written his 'Saints
Everlasting Rest'.

Middle Littleton has a church of mixed styles with a Norman font,
a beautiful seventeenth-century manor house and an outstanding
tithe barn of the Abbots of Evesham which dates from 1260. It is
reminiscent of the great barn at Bredon. South Littleton again is a
church of all periods and a Norman font with tapering sides like its
neighbour at Middle. The fine brick house called Hathaways
opposite the church should be noticed. It looks like a Caroline house,
but there is the date 1721 on the weathervane; other parts are
Elizabethan and even earlier. The cupola and the two broad chimney
stacks with the open arch joining them make a striking architectural
device. Bretforton, a somewhat larger village, has a church which, so
the architectural experts insist, owes the inspiration of its early
thirteenth-century arcade to work in Wells Cathedral. It would be
interesting to discover what the connection might have been. The
chancel is late thirteenth-century work and the nave and tower
Perpendicular. The Manor House is a typical Jacobean three-gabled
structure, but we liked better Bretforton Hall which is 'Strawberry
Hill Gothic' of late eighteenth or early nineteenth century construc-

tion. With its ogee-headed windows and tower with battlements it certainly looks the kind of house where Jane Austen's characters might have lived. The timbered Fleece hostelry near by has a fine collection of old furniture and pewter.

Cleeve Prior is a pleasant village with cottages grouped round a green, a heavily Victorianised church with the usual range of architectural periods and a beautiful late sixteenth-century manor house with a round dovecote. Badsey church, restored in 1885, retains a good 1617 monument to Richard Hoby and his kneeling children and there are several houses in the village, sixteenth and seventeenth century and Georgian periods, and an interesting vicarage built two or three years ago showing the kind of accommodation now provided for the clergy who have been shouting out for years that their houses are too big. They had every reason for shouting at Offenham, where another modern vicarage has recently replaced a quite horrid early nineteenth-century house. The church here is another effort of the prolific Preedy from 1861, but it retains a fifteenth-century tower. And the village boasts a permanent maypole which is a pleasant innovation which should be more common in country villages; also the grandest Royal British Legion Club in which the writer has ever had the good fortune to be entertained.

It is not necessary to return from Evesham to Worcester along the usual A44 road through Pershore. Near the station there runs off another, B4084, which passes through Moor and sufficiently near Cropthorne and Throckmorton and Fladbury and Pinvin to give us a sight of some interesting buildings along that alternative route. First, in the parish of Fladbury, there is Craycombe House, a plain and rather severe composition of 1791 built by a returned Indian nabob, George Perrott, with George Byfield the architect. This house may be easily visited as it is a restaurant and country club. Its additional interest arises from the fact that it was the home of Francis Brett Young. We have deplored the paucity of Worcestershire novelists, but here was a master indeed who knew his county and its people through and through and did much to interpret them to the world. Some of his Worcestershire stories and perhaps his South African ones too, will have a lasting place on the shelf of outstanding twentieth-century novels. Near to Craycombe is Woodnorton, where once lived the Duc d'Orléans and where, in the chapel, the Duc's sister married Prince Charles of Bourbon in 1907. This house is now one of the establishments of the B.B.C.

Fladbury has much charm. Its mill, by the lock, is picturesque and still contains machinery, but the 1710 rectory, which Pevsner describes in some detail in 1968, suffered a severe fire, stood derelict for some years and has now completely given place to a small housing estate. But the church is a joy and a generous and specific benefaction for the maintenance of the churchyard a few years ago allows it to be maintained in a setting of impeccable tidiness. The lower part of the tower is Norman but it was heightened and the church otherwise altered about 1300 with Decorated and Perpendicular work coming later. There is an extremely precious bit of early fourteenth-century glass here of the Virgin and Child. So fine is this specimen that it was thought fit to exhibit it in Paris a year or two ago where it attracted most favourable attention. The memorial brasses here, especially the 1445 representation of John Throckmorton and his wife are among the best in the County. And the mention of this couple had better lead us on to Throckmorton, their place of origin, where a little 'hedge church' of the thirteenth and fourteenth centuries still maintains a resistance to a threat of redundancy. There is a fine timbered house of 1500 at Court Farm. But the story of the Throckmorton family, an important story, moves to Warwickshire where their principal residence in post-Reformation times, Coughton Court, should most certainly be visited.

Finally, there is Cropthorne, one of the show villages of the County with a long straggling street which runs parallel with the Avon and a variety of pretty houses, timbered and brick. Among these, the Old House, having a nucleus of genuine early timbered construction, a great deal of extension in the same style and a recent chapel by Maurice Jones in an idiom so completely up to date that its arches have the faintest suggestion of a new Gothic, deserves special mention as being the well-used Retreat and Conference House of the Worcester Diocese. Cropthorne Church, like nearby Fladbury, has an unbuttressed Norman tower and other Norman features overlaid by thirteenth-century and other later building. A find, rare for Worcestershire, is to be seen here, an Anglo-Saxon cross head decorated with birds and beasts. It dates from the second quarter of the ninth century. The memorial to Francis Dineley and his wife of 1624 is not likely to be missed, set somewhat uncomfortably as it is across the chancel arch.

We have strayed a little from our main homeward route in order to visit these last notable villages; so now on through Moor and Wyre Piddle, where we have not time to linger though the latter has a Norman church. Our road is now a straight open way which passes through no more villages though Pinvin, Peopleton and White Ladies Aston lie to the east and may be reserved for another excursion. Our road meets the main Worcester–Alcester road a little to the east of Spetchley and a sharp left turn here leads us in the course of a few miles back to the city which we enter along the London Road from which we began.

CHAPTER FIVE

East and North-East towards Warwickshire

An exploration of the north-eastern section of the County is best undertaken along two spokes which leave Worcester, one from the roundabout at the junction of the London and Whittington roads, travelling directly east until it quickly reaches the Warwickshire border at Alcester, the other taking the north-east road to the right at the Barbourne fork and travelling on through Droitwich and Broms-grove until it enters the Birmingham suburbs at Rubery. Between the termini of these spokes is the rapidly expanding town of Redditch.

Along the first and eastern spoke the first stopping place of interest is Spetchley, the territory of the important historic family of Berkeley. The descent of the Berkeley properties is a curious one. The last Lord Berkeley, who spent a fortune on restoring Berkeley Castle, died without a direct heir. In order to discover a new owner the family pedigree had to be investigated a considerable distance back and the Worcestershire Berkeleys of Spetchley became the new owners, thus combining one of the best money-spinners in the stately home business in the medieval castle in Gloucestershire with the rather prim though spacious and dignified Regency mansion in Worcester-shire. This is a neo-classic building by Tasker of 1811, replacing a previous house which was Cromwell's headquarters during the Battle of Worcester in 1651. The house is rarely exhibited to the public but frequent access is granted to the grounds, which have been laid out with conspicuous skill and are particularly a riot of spring flowers. The Berkeleys have always been a steadfast Recusant family and their Roman Catholic Chapel is within the house, but their family memorials, Jacobean and of a high quality, are in the Anglican

Church on the main road on the fringe of the park. The bulk of the church dates from the sixteenth and seventeenth centuries and the Berkeley Chapel where the monuments are disposed is 1614. The Catholic village school on the other side of the road is one of the few A. W. Pugin buildings in the County; it is a plain unassuming structure and adds little lustre to his name.

Between here and the Warwickshire border we have a series of villages whose double-barrelled names trip mellifluously from the tongue: Broughton Hackett, Upton Snodsbury, Grafton Flyford, Flyford Flavell, Naunton Beauchamp and the Peopleton and White Ladies Aston which lay on our right as we travelled to Worcester along the 'back way' from Evesham. Here also is a Churchill, one of two in the County—the other lies a little to the north of Kidderminster—but neither, as far as we know, has any connection with the famous family. White Ladies Aston, prettily so named, took its origin from a manor which the White Ladies of Worcester, with their priory on the site of the modern Boys' Grammar School, held here in the middle of the thirteenth century. The church is of Norman origin and has a tall timbered bell turret and spire which may be as early as the nave. Peopleton's special feature is the beautifully carved beam with a leaf frieze which is part of the former rood screen and there is a good Jacobean communion rail.

The remaining villages which flank this main road each have their simple and unassuming churches and houses about which there is little that is remarkable. Crowle, largely rebuilt by Preedy in 1881, possesses, however, a most important stone lectern which bears comparison with the lectern at Norton. It has, apparently, been drastically restored, probably in 1845 when it was retrieved from the churchyard. Italian in sentiment it is nevertheless English, with a kneeling man holding vine tendrils, and dates from about 1200. These is considerable probability that, like the Norton lectern, it came from Evesham Abbey. A memorial tablet to the late Col. Davison of Froxmere Court and also of Thorngrove Hallow is a good piece of modern craftsmanship with a coloured heraldic achievement and excellent lettering. The north porch is also a relic of the former fourteenth-century church. It is heavily timbered and the wooden boss within and the carving of the Annunciation above the entrance are quite noteworthy. Churchill, its church dating from the fourteenth century and badly restored in 1863, also possesses what is rare in Worcestershire, a fine and large water mill which has recently been restored and adapted as a dwelling house by one of the County's foremost architects.

Broughton Hackett's small church is thirteenth-century work, largely rebuilt, with a western wooden tower and two pre-Reformation bells. Upton Snodsbury with a Perpendicular tower, for the rest, is mostly restoration by W. J. Hopkins in 1873, but the Perpendicular font with its symbols of the Evangelists is of some interest. Hopkins seems to have been much sought after in this neighbourhood for at Grafton Flyford he restored the fourteenth-century church in 1875 and at Flyford Flavell in 1883. It is still possible in all these heavily restored buildings for the antiquarian enthusiast to pick out details which are of interest, bits of ancient glass, seventeenth- and eighteenth-century monuments, fifteenth-century tiles and invariably there is some good plate, often dating from that important year 1571 when a large number of cups and cover patens demonstrate a burst of Elizabethan activity to replace the ravages of the Reformation plunder. Similarly at Naunton Beauchamp we have a fourteenth-century church restoration, again by Hopkins in 1897, and the features here are a 1550 pulpit and a Jacobean communion rail. The searcher will also find some beautiful timbered and stone houses, perhaps originally of superior status but now mostly farms, as at Naunton Court, Rectory Farm and Hill Court at Grafton Flyford, Churchill Farm at Churchill, Aston Hill at White Ladies Aston and Norchard House and White House at Peopleton. The timber-framed towers of the churches at Dormston and Kington, reminiscent of Pirton, pose the problem of difficult dating which is inherent in all timbered buildings, but the closeness of the timbers indicates, as we have suggested earlier, at least fourteenth- or fifteenth-century date.

When we reach Inkberrow, a much bigger village, we seem to be in an entirely different world, for although it is still a village, it is a very large village which has expanded with much residential building in the last few years and it is already beginning to assume the attitudes of commuter suburbia. But it is still a pleasant place. If we are a little tired of over-much ecclesiology we can relax in the luxury of the

Old Bull Hotel and stimulate our imagination by the knowledge that this is indeed the true and only original of the Bull Hotel at Ambridge. It can easily be peopled by the characters who have entertained us for so many years at 6.45 p.m. on Radio 4 and it takes no long stretch of alcoholic fancy to perceive Walter Gabriel or Tom Forrest trotting in and out of a very small room quite properly inscribed 'COLTS' in careful distinction from its neighbour 'FILLIES'. But the more sober minded will certainly wish to visit the church, which records a very singular *'lapsus memoriae'*. For here King Charles I left his maps and the vicar assures us that they are safely locked up in the vestry safe awaiting collection on the appropriate Judgment Day. A glance at the church itself shows a building of which the oldest part is Perpendicular; there are Georgian and Victorian additions. And on the north side there are pinnacles and battlements and a porch with large gargoyles which the visitor, however long may have been his session at the Old Bull, must never suppose have been placed there by grateful villagers as a pictorial tribute to the fame which the Archers have brought them.

We are getting close to Redditch now which is a bit of our industrial fringe or rather a tassel hanging from it, for we are still well to the south of Birmingham; but the 'great wen' is steadily spreading and may some day quite engulf all this neighbourhood. Already the Redditch Development Corporation are expanding the town with a vast new housing development which shows every refinement of modern planning. Between Inkberrow and Redditch there are Feckenham and Astwood Bank to be visited, travelling north along a road which runs literally along the Warwickshire border.

What has become of the once important royal forest which took its name from Feckenham? When the great forest land of Worcestershire began to contract there still remained Wyre Forest and the jealously preserved Malvern Chase and Feckenham forest with a village at its heart and a manor house, much favoured as a hunting lodge in the twelfth and thirteenth centuries and bought by the abbots of Evesham in 1356. There is no trace of it now due no doubt to the activities of the Droitwich salt boilers, but the High Street has some fine timbered and Georgian houses and the church retains some Perpendicular and Early English work, though Butterfield added a chancel in 1853, and Day of Worcester rebuilt the south wall of the nave in 1866. Astwood Bank is an industrial place of recent growth and its church was the work of W. J. Hopkins in 1884 with the nave built by Cogswell in 1911. Then we pass through Crabbs Cross into the growing town of Redditch.

If it did not bespeak a too uncomfortable posture one might say, in Leland's phrase, 'Redditch standeth upon needles and fish hooks'. Did the industry first originate at nearby Bordesley Abbey to give the monks a financial fillip as with the tiles at Malvern? In the Middle Ages Redditch was mostly Bordesley Abbey, a Cistercian house of 1138 foundation with 33 monks in 1332 and 19 in 1381. We are gradually getting to know a good deal more about this place, for careful and scientific excavation has been going on there in recent years and the records of the newly discovered shapes of the buildings are most illuminating. At any rate, at the Dissolution the monks departed but the needles remained. There were 400 people employed in the industry in 1782 and there are about 2,000 now. But whatever development may do for Redditch we hope that it will not touch that central square which some might say was the only redeeming feature of a somewhat drab place. Church Green, as it is called, is dominated by Woodyer's very large decorated St. Stephen's Church of 1854; there was more intelligent work done in the chancel by Temple Moore, one of the greatest of the later neo-Gothic architects in 1873. There are tiles from Bordesley Abbey in the vestry and some stained glass by Kempe. A few Georgian houses line Prospect Hill but there are no buildings of much architectural interest in the town and even Rickman, of whom we can generally expect something fairly exciting in the early phases of the Gothic revival, is rather disappointing with his Roman Catholic Our Lady of Mount Carmel, 1834. St. George's, the other Anglican church, is again the ubiquitous Preedy giving us a rather dull church of 1876 in the thirteenth-century idiom.

But at Beoley, a little outside the town, we really do encounter a church which is quite exciting. It begins in the twelfth century, has a south and north arcade of around 1300 and a west tower and north aisle in the Perpendicular style. There are interesting furnishings in the church, but the most important associations are with the Sheldon chapel on the north side which dates from the late sixteenth century.

Here are two fine Elizabethan and Jacobean monuments, the former to William Sheldon and his wife, about 1570, and the latter to Ralph Sheldon and his wife, about 1613. Mrs. Esdaile has no mention of these monuments, which is disappointing for there is a fine array of stone achievements here and much heraldry and many wall tablets. The interest of the Sheldon family, of course, is that they were the originators of tapestry weaving in England. The art had apparently been learned in Flanders by Richard Hickes whom William had sent there and whom he describes in his will as 'the only author and beginner of tapestry and arras within this realm'. The tapestries were made at Barcheston in Warwickshire and also, Pevsner says, at Bordesley. The tapestry maps, collected at Barcheston, were dispersed at the end of the eighteenth century. It has been stated, though we cannot trace the evidence, that Horace Walpole bought a large number of them, and there are certainly some in the Victoria and Albert Museum and in the Birmingham Barber Institute.

Whilst Beoley remains still a fringe village of Redditch, though who knows for how much longer, the new town has already engulfed Ipsley, which has a Perpendicular parish church which lost its aisles in 1785; but it retains a big fourteenth-century font and an ornate Elizabethan pulpit which came from Easton in Herefordshire. The Hubands were the family here with their monuments in the church and a portion of their late seventeenth-century house, Ipsley Court, still surviving. The late Georgian rectory has been transmogrified from a ministerial residence to a social club.

Northwards beyond Redditch is Alvechurch, now very much Birmingham suburban. The bishops of Worcester had a house here which was demolished in 1780 and the church looks a curious proposition. This is because Butterfield in 1859 built a tall nave against a remaining tower of a previous building. There is a Norman south doorway and a thirteenth-century chancel and the tower is 1676. But the Victorian work here is of great interest, perhaps one of the best ecclesiastical Gothic Revival specimens in the County. Butterfield, at his best, was a very great architect, instance Keble College and All Saints, Margaret Street; a large and important book on his work recently published witnesses to a growing appreciation of his achievements. Here he has given us something quite characteristic, constructive coloration and all; medieval effigies to a knight and a Worcester fifteenth-century bishop look a trifle uneasy in these surroundings. But Butterfield certainly designed here some of the best of his medievalism as he interpreted it. He also built for the rector of 1872 a fine brick and half-timbered house, but the present rector no longer inhabits it. The schools too are Butterfield of 1856 and there is Lewknor's Hospital founded in 1588 by the generosity of Nicholas Lewknor of Haseley in Oxfordshire. Lewknor in 1580 left two-thirds of his estate in Hadzor to his relative Thomas Copley, whom we have already met as the builder of Bredon's Norton Manor, on condition that part of the income should be used to build and endow an almshouse at Alvechurch. Copley discharged his trust and in 1588 built upon two acres of land a hospital for a master, six brethren and two sisters. The Hospital still stands, though the present dwellings look more like a later rebuilding than a construction of the period of Copley.

There remains now to describe the link between these two spokes, a great house and an impressive Georgian church. The latter is Tardebigge built by Francis Hiorn in 1777, though the chancel is a Victorian addition of 1879. There is a most impressive Georgian tower and spire and we can enjoy Lady Mary Cooke's monument and Chantrey's 1835 memorial to the 6th Earl of Plymouth; a magnificent *art nouveau* lectern by the Bromsgrove Guild is a unique possession. There was a medieval church here of the twelfth century and it is related that the chancel was in Warwickshire and the nave in Worcestershire. So scrupulous, so it is said, was Thomas Habington who, after his hairbreadth escape from disaster following the Powder Plot, had given his word never to quit his native county, that when he came to survey Tardebigge he described only the nave for fear of putting a foot into Warwickshire.

At Hewell Grange we have something that is rare in Worcestershire, a great country house, built by truly great modern architects. The house was the seat of the Earls of Plymouth, who now no longer live there for it is a Borstal institution. The architects are Bodley and Garner; the date 1884. The general impression of this huge house is adapted Jacobean and its principal feature is a vast entrance hall which occupies half the house. Two stories in height, it abounds in columns and galleries, reached by a wide Jacobean-type staircase. The chapel too has a touch of the exotic with marble and lapis lazuli; another notable late Victorian architect is responsible here, Detmar Blow. It must have been a most extraordinary house in which to live. Surviving tapestries in the Great Hall in the French Romance mode, *à la* William Morris, and pieces of Medieval glass inserted in the chapel windows are a surprising find.

We return to Worcester and set out again to explore the north-easterly direction of the County along the spoke which takes the right hand fork at Barbourne in north Worcester. A glance to the right as we leave the town shows us the two stone columns which, with a stable block are all that remain of the demolished Perdiswell Hall. But they deserve a note for they carry two sculptured panels of Coade stone which are rare in the County, though there is an urn on one of the gate piers at Croome and urns in the niches, and on the parapet and on the wall roundels of Byfield's 1791 Craycombe House. In the fork between this right-hand Droitwich Road and the left-hand Ombersley road lies the parish of Claines, highly favoured suburban Worcester. Its church is Perpendicular, but the clever Aston Webb has been here and left us, in 1886, a very good north aisle and north porch. This church is very well known to Worcester people, largely, if the truth be told, because of the popular hostelry, the Mug, which stands almost in the churchyard.

Porters Mill, in this parish, is an important early sixteenth-century timbered house. Its claim to be one of the many places in which Queen Elizabeth slept away from home seems to be better substantiated than most. The Queen visited here on 14 August 1575, on her way from Hartlebury to Worcester. It is stated that the panelled bedroom in which she slept was specially decorated with a fine plaster ceiling and that the royal cipher, E.R., and the Royal Coat of Arms were set up over the fireplace in the hall and never removed. The parish of Claines had to provide 24 fowl and she was presented with a gold cup worth £40 and a velvet purse containing £20. It is claimed that a chalice, still in use at Claines church, was presented by the Queen.

But returning to the Droitwich road and passing through Fernhill

Heath we see on high ground to the left the picturesque group of buildings, church, rectory and farm which make up Martin Hussing-tree. The church is Norman with a side aisle of 1883, the rectory is eighteenth-century brickwork and the brick Court Farm is seventeenth century. This is the burial place of Thomas Tomkins, who for so long sustained the music of the Cathedral. He was organist and choir master for 53 years, but his reign terminated when the Puritans discontinued musical services there during the Commonwealth. He was born at St. Davids in 1572 and was buried here in 1656, having lived his last sad years at the Court whose wealthy owner was the wife of his son Nathaniel.

On the other side of the main road is Hindlip Hall, an entirely rebuilt, rather grim, Victorian mansion, now the headquarters of the West Mercia Constabulary. It seems a poor exchange for the great Elizabethan house of the Habingtons which figured so prominently in Worcestershire conspiratorial history. We have a print of that house in Nash's *Worcestershire* and other drawings made in 1814 when the house was being pulled down; and Mr. Michael Hodgetts, our Catholic historian, has faithfully recorded for us in the Transactions of the County Archaeological Society a most useful account of the Hall and the ingenious hiding holes for fugitive priests which it contained. Prattinton, who knew it just before it was pulled down, supplies much of our evidence about what must have been a head-quarters of what Mr. Hodgetts calls 'the Jesuit underground between 1590 and 1606'. The place where faithful priests were hunted has now become the headquarters for the hunt for twentieth-century criminals in this area.

Further along the main road on the left taking the turn at the curiously named Copcut Elm Inn we travel to the village of Sal-warpe which possesses what is externally one of the finest of our timbered houses. It dates from about 1500 and was a home of the Talbot family. Richard Beauchamp, Earl of Warwick was born here. Some of its details, particularly on the south-west or solar side are extremely good, but the interior contains little of outstanding interest. The church which is mostly Perpendicular contains some good monuments, one to a later fourteenth-century priest and others to members of the Talbot family.

144

23 *(opposite) Evesham – Abbot Lichfield's Campanile*

Droitwich, in spite of its well-known name, is a somewhat disappointing and featureless place. It has a great antiquity and appears now to be on the threshold of a prosperous future with its current development as an overspill town; building goes furiously ahead. Droitwich, of course, has always owed its fame to salt. Perhaps the Romans knew about it, for a villa has been excavated here and certainly Domesday Book recorded its salt pans. But travellers agreed until the early nineteenth century that it was mean and dirty. But in 1828, as today, it was evident that a more exciting future was in store for it, for in that year the maker of modern Droitwich, John Corbett, opened his Stoke Prior Salt Works and at Droitwich began a series of building exploits most of which still survive. The Raven Hotel is reputed to embody the old Manor House of the town and the curious may like the exercise of disentangling what is genuine and what is imitation in the timbering. The Worcestershire Hotel is enormous and seems now to subsist on luncheon conferences for businessmen of nearby industrial areas. This was not always so, for indeed until very recently these and other hotels were the places where the wealthy patients stayed who had come to Droitwich to partake of the brine baths treatment. The mechanism of the cure seems to have been somewhat different from the Spartan regime of the water-cure as imposed at Malvern. Could it really have been true, as the proprietors of the Royal Baths said, that here was the strongest water in Europe, 12 times stronger than sea water and 40% more dense than the Red Sea? At all events it is a singular experience to try a total immersion in the brine bath; one dare hardly call it a swimming bath and certainly you must not dive into it. It is all you can do to prevent your feet floating up to the surface and perhaps it is as well to cling to the rails at the side of the bath. But at any rate you will never drown there: that would be a physical impossibility. But the popularity of the baths seems to be becoming rather a thing of the past and no longer do we observe the elegant if arthritic ladies and gentlemen occupying their tables in the dining room of the Worcestershire Hotel as we did a few years ago. There are nursing homes and a hospital to cater for less opulent sufferers, but, all in all, we get the impression that this aspect of the historic Droitwich is on the way out.

It would be a pity to miss the fantastic house which the salt king

24 (*opposite above*) *Bretforton – The Fleece*
25 (*below*) *Ombersley – a 'black and white' village*

built for his French wife, who, if rumour be correct, refused to live there. It could not have been through any lack of effort to make the house look as French as possible, for though John Corbett may have called his house Impney Manor, no one in Worcestershire would think of calling it anything but Château Impney. It was begun in 1869 and its architect, Tronquois, was a Parisian. It has all the hall-marks of a towering French château, brick and stone mixed, deep *porte-cochère*, steep roofs and very large dormer windows. Its only function today could be as a hotel or country club and management after management has tried in recent years to make it pay, but with small success. Now again (1972) vast sums have been spent on restoration and redecoration and yet another start has been made. We wish it well for we believe that our Worcestershire countryside would be the poorer for the passing of this incongruous *folie de grandeur*; it is quite ridiculous, we know, but Worcestershire people have a sneaking fondness for its absurdity.

We return to the town to glean what few antiquarian bits remain and they of course are in three of the four churches. St. Andrew's, which comes very close upon the main street, is a curiously jumbled building of all periods from the early thirteenth century to a north aisle of about 1910. One gets the impression here that the bits and pieces have somehow not been very skilfully put together, but there are some finely carved capitals and a delicious little Jacobean font and cover. St. Peter's, across the fields, a mile from the old town but now thickly encompassed with new housing, is a pleasant church with a Norman chancel complete with three small windows and a Norman chancel arch. There are transepts of later periods and a south aisle of the thirteenth century and in the decorated north transept, rather splendidly coloured in red, lies George Wylde, Sergeant at law who died in 1616. Edward Winslow, one of the *Mayflower* pioneers and later Governor of Massachusetts, is commemorated here and there is a Nash tablet of 1690, reminding us that part of the celebrated and wide-spreading county family of Nash lived at the pleasant half-timbered St. Peter's Manor near the church. As you leave the church you must not look back; the appropriate text 'Remember Lot's wife' inscribed over the porch reminds you that you stand over salt brine in which curious things may happen.

Standing on a hill, towering above the town, is the church of Dodderhill. 'Towering' is the right word, for the building is dominated by an enormous tower built in 1708. It is reputed that this replaces a tower which was taken down after the Civil War. There is no nave, but there is a long north transept of the early nineteenth century and there is a re-set window in the transept which corresponds with the chancel east window of 1322 when it is known that new altars in the church were dedicated. The north wall of the chancel is again of early nineteenth-century brick, so, once more, we have to say that the whole thing is a jumble, but this time a jumble which somehow or another seems congruous and right. It is certainly a very attractive church.

There are two other little churches to the south of Droitwich which should be visited, Oddingley especially to see its stained glass, a good deal of it with saints motifs of about 1500. The building itself is a wholesale restoration by R. C. Hussey of 1851, but a wooden arch to the south transept with an entrance to rood loft stairs still survives. Once a parson of Oddingley was murdered and there was a bit of mystery connected with his death. Whether it was a matter of tithe resentment is obscure; it is one of our classic Worcestershire scandals, but too long and involved to relate here. The other church is Hadzor, Decorated in style and restored last in 1866, perhaps by Street. It stands hard by the great house of the Galton family, a distinguished name in the world of science, which was built originally in 1779 but enormously enlarged in 1827 in the Grecian taste, and latterly doing service as a Roman Catholic seminary. Some thirty years ago the Anglican clergyman was a gentleman known to his brethren as 'Raban of Hadzor', which always seemed as delightful an Old Testament evocation as might be conceived. But Mr. Raban has long been dead and his church, alas, is yet another that has been declared redundant.

On the west side of Droitwich and on the right-hand side of the road to Ombersley, leaving the newly developing part of the town behind us we follow an immensely long brick wall towards the appropriate entrance gates. The wall seems to promise something rather grand and important and we are not to be disappointed. For behind it lies the park and house of Westwood, one of the most curious and significant great houses of the County. Westwood deserves much longer description than can be afforded here, but if access can be gained, and bear in mind that it is now divided into a number of self-contained flats, it is a treat indeed. The house stands on the site of a Benedictine Nunnery, granted to the Pakington family after the Dissolution. They came from Hampton Lovett, not far away, but when the house there was burnt in the Civil War Sir John enlarged a hunting lodge which *his* grandfather John had built at the end of the sixteenth century, by adding wings which are the distinctive feature of the house. These date from early Restoration times and are fixed diagonally at the angles of the old hunting lodge. Hence, then, the curious X shape, emphasised by the great height and the elaborately shaped gables and parapets with strapwork and carving. Within lies a Great Hall and impressive staircase and, grandest of all, the Great Chamber with elaborate chimney piece, frieze and ceiling. The last private owner, before the flats came, was Lord Doverdale, but the name which haunts this splendid pile is, of course, Pakington.

The first Sir John, who secured the dissolved nunnery, was one of Henry VIII's favourite lawyers who may have been active in 'the King's matter' which precipitated the Reformation. The family persevered in the public service and another Sir John so pleased Queen Elizabeth with his athletic prowess that she named him 'Lusty Pakington'. In the eighteenth century another Sir John, elected member of Parliament for Worcester, at the age of 19, held tight to his seat until his death except that he declined the position in the parliament of 1695–8. In modern times a Pakington was a member of Disraeli's Cabinet and earned the ennobling of the family after these hundreds of years of public service as the first Baron Hampton, deriving his title from the family's earliest home.

Happily, Lord Hampton, grandson of the Victorian statesman, is still with us, one of the most venerated figures in the County, paying his service to Church and State in many diverse ways. He is a man of incredible versatility, sailor, architect, man of letters and novelist who, under the name of Humphrey Pakington, has given us a series of the most delightful whimsical novels about Worcestershire, from which some of its inhabitants have extracted great pleasure or anger in imagining themselves as having been the subjects of some of the characters portrayed. He is also a distinguished antiquary who, with his son, the Hon. Richard Pakington, has recently revised one of the better known County books and we have good hope that before long we may have from their pen a chronicle of the Pakington family history which will undoubtedly be an enrichment of the historical records of the County. Lord Hampton entirely disclaims the notion that his ancestor, the long-sitting Parliamentarian of the eighteenth century, was the original of Addison's 'Sir Roger de Coverley', as has sometimes been alleged.

The Pakington family memorials are not far away in the Norman church of Hampton Lovett and among them is Dr. Hammond, chaplain to Charles I, who found sanctuary at Westwood, as did at a later date, the dispossessed, non-juring George Hickes, Dean of Worcester, continuing the reputation of that great house as a strong-hold of High Church Anglicanism.

We must travel on now from Droitwich in a north-easterly direction along the road which leads to Bromsgrove. Wychbold, Elmbridge and Upton Warren lie a little to the west of the road. Wychbold has a big Victorian church of 1888 built by John Corbett; there is a thirteenth-century doorway and what appears to be an original window in the south-east Decorated tower. Elmbridge was mostly rebuilt in 1872 but retains a late Norman south doorway and a thirteenth-century north arcade. Upton Warren has relics of all centuries from a tower of the mid-thirteenth to a chancel, possibly of seventeenth-century origin, rebuilt in 1724 and a nave with west gallery of 1798. The east window of 1880 has been described, not by us, as 'uncommonly horrible'.

Hanbury, to the east of this main road but further south and nearer Droitwich must certainly not be overlooked, for Hanbury Hall possesses a unique treasure and as the house is now in the possession of the National Trust there are facilities for viewing it at stated times. It seems a far cry from St. Paul's Cathedral to mid-Worcestershire but the same artist has been at work in both places and the treasure is a staircase decorated by no less an artist than Thornhill in about 1710. There are classical scenes set in an architectural framework and a cherub holds a portrait of the notorious Dr. Sacheverell which is to be torn by furies. The owners here must have been very much in touch with the events of a larger world and no doubt Thomas

Vernon, barrister, would be well aware of crucial issues concerning religious freedom which were involved in the trial of the rascally doctor. This is a magnificent house, the nearest we possess to a Wren house, built around 1700 and the name of the celebrated architect Talman has been suggested in connection with it. But this is guess-work based on similarities to other known work by Talman. The architect was, in fact, William Rudhall of Henley-in-Arden and the house is certainly one of the County's most precious architectural treasures. It is good to know that it is in safe hands.

The Vernons were a most distinguished Worcestershire family and their fortunes, like the Coventry family fortunes, were based on the law. But collateral branches were widespread and they also served the Church, for Vernon names appear among the rectors of Shrawley and Martley and Areley Kings. A symposium of the family history of this branch may be found in the church, where most of the monuments are to Vernons; the sculptors include some famous names like Roubiliac and Chantrey. It is quite evident that in death the family were determined to have the best that could be obtained in that line.

The church perches on top of a hill and externally was rebuilt in the late eighteenth century though there is medieval work within. The south arcade is about 1210 and the north arcade Perpendicular. Then came a Victorian addition and it is interesting to see what a first-rate Victorian architect could do when he was entrusted with the enlarging of a medieval church. The architect was George E. Street, a name distinguished enough, and we have disappointingly little of his work in Worcestershire. He rebuilt the chancel and the Vernon chapel in 1860 and though some authorities think that he was not at his best at Hanbury to us it seems a pretty convincing piece of work.

The Victorian rectory at the foot of the hill at the east of the church was built by David Brandon in 1862. It can only be described as gargantuan and a relic of an age of wealthy clergy and modestly paid servants. As a clerical habitation in these days its future is likely to be short-lived. But in these rigidly controlled green belt areas it is extremely difficult to find suitable and permitted sites on which to rehouse the clergy in even a modest fashion. G. E. Street was also responsible for the village school in 1860.

There is also a most important timbered house near here, Mere

Hall, which in spite of an optimistic 1337 on a bracket, is not likely to go much further back than the mid-sixteenth century. It has some pretty features, especially the five little gables with finials in the middle and the Gothick glazing bars which were the contribution of an early Victorian restoring architect, probably Matthew Habershon who designed Hadzor House, to the perpetuating of a Tudor idiom.

Now one of our larger towns claims our attention. Bromsgrove had early connections with the clothing trade, as Leland reminds us; it might also have developed into another Redditch because, before the end of the eighteenth century, nail-making was carried on, as at Redditch, from the homes of the people. But ultimately its prosperity came to depend upon its position as the centre of an agricultural area and it is still, paramountly, a market town retaining its market place surrounded by some fine timbered houses and, as in Leland's time, a very long main street. Fortunately it also retains a very magnificent parish church, one of the finest and biggest of our Worcestershire churches, restored but not rebuilt and standing on such high ground that it truly dominates the town. It also possesses what is uncommon in our county, a splendid tapering spire set on a fourteenth-century tower, complete with three niches containing figures. The oldest parts are a twelfth-century south doorway, a thirteenth-century south aisle and a fifteenth-century north aisle. It contains some most important monuments, including on the north wall of the chancel, the tomb of Elizabeth, the first wife of Sir Gilbert Talbot who received the important manor of Grafton in 1486, and, in the north aisle the tomb of Sir John Talbot, Gilbert's son, and his two wives. Sir John is heavily armoured and his ladies attired in a fashion which gives us valuable information about the costume of the sixteenth century. This tomb with its family reminiscences played its part in a famous *cause celèbre* of 1856 when, by removing paint which covered the evidence, links were found to establish the claim of Lord Talbot of Ingestre to the Earldom of Shrewsbury. There is also the tomb of Humphrey Stafford of Grafton whose son, also Humphrey, had fought for Richard at Bosworth and was later executed for high treason. The father, whose monument we have here, had also come to a violent end, for he was killed in Jack Cade's rebellion. But this is only a small selection of the memorials which have survived in an unusually large number in this notable church.

While the Talbots of Grafton are still in our mind it should be recorded that Grafton Manor still stands, about a mile and a half south-west of Bromsgrove. A good deal of it dates from the 1860s and is the work of the David Brandon whom we met at Hanbury Rectory. But there is some of John Talbot's work of 1567 still surviving and the main porch to the house is remarkable as a classic piece of Renaissance architecture complete with Doric columns. This house, of great tradition, still performs a useful function as an old people's home.

To many Worcestershire people, especially the richer farmers, Bromsgrove is an honoured name by reason of the school at which their sons were educated. Like so many of these well-known schools which attained great prosperity in the last century—and many of them continued it into this—it began in the church, as a school conducted by a priest of the Stafford Chantry. It was fortunate in its acquisition of large new endowments which were given to it in 1693 by Sir Thomas Cookes, founder of Worcester College, Oxford. The oldest school building on the main road with the Cookes arms is a charming period house of 1695, but it deceptively hides a wide-spreading campus behind it and a huge complex of school buildings of Victorian (1850) date onwards. One of the most recent and perhaps most interesting is Sir Giles G. Scott's chapel of 1928, completed only in 1958.

One of Bromsgrove's most cherished names is that of A. E. Housman, born at Fockbury a mile or two away from the town. His family lived for five years at the Clock House and the boy won a Foundation Scholarship to the Bromsgrove School at the age of eleven. But it is a mistake to suppose that he was forever resting on hill tops and dreaming of 'coloured counties'. In spite of early frustrations and disappointments he eventually carved out for himself a great reputation in the field of somewhat recondite classical scholarship. It is likely that he himself was well aware of the aridity of his chosen profession for somewhere he wrote: 'A scholar who means to build himself a monument must spend much of his life in acquiring knowledge which for its own sake is not worth having and in reading books which do not in themselves deserve to be read.' A devastating dictum, and yet perhaps a self-revelation of the tremendous weight of discipline which he imposed upon himself to repress a deeply emotional nature whose only escape from bondage was when it burst out in those romantic lyrics, perhaps among the loveliest of this century, in *A Shropshire Lad*.

Finstall, a district of Bromsgrove, was originally a chapelry of Stoke Prior. Its ancient church was replaced by a plain Georgian brick building of 1773 which stood derelict for many years until it was finally demolished in 1971; a church of 1883 by John Cotton had taken its place. It contains a striking piece of carved stone work by Pancheri, commemorating the D-day landings of 6 June 1944, which was the day of the church's patron, St. Godwald. This name is probably the most interesting thing about Finstall Church, for it shares with Chaddesley Corbett the distinction of possessing a patronal dedication which is unique in England. But who was Godwald or Gudwal and why should we encounter him here? According to Miss Margaret Deanesly he was an abbot-bishop of about 500 A.D. with a monastery of clergy on an island on the southern coast of Brittany. There appears to have been something of a unique devotion to this saint in Worcestershire, for a few fragments of fourteenth-century stone piers in the garden of the Commandery in Worcester are the remains of the chapel of the hospital which was founded there by St. Wulfstan in 1085 and which may have been dedicated in honour of St. Godwald. A representation of him appears among the mural paintings in the house. The Cathedral, according to Domesday Book, owned land in Stoke Prior. Miss Deanesly suggests that relics of St. Godwald might have been passed on, presumably from the Cathedral to Stoke Prior and thence to Finstall. Why St. Godwald in Worcestershire? We venture a suggestion. Was he the patron saint of St. Wulfstan?

Dodford is a church unique in Worcestershire, for it is our only specimen of an Arts and Crafts enterprise of the early twentieth century. It vies with Kempley in Gloucestershire and Brockhampton in Herefordshire. Its architect, Arthur Bartlett, who designed it in 1908, was a pupil of Blomfield and was responsible for other work at Bromsgrove School and Hartlebury Castle. The relationship of the church and the massive tower at the south end of the transept, the enclosing east–west cloister and the outside pulpit in the courtyard are clever features, the tower with its saddleback roof and structured cross between the twin upper windows is striking. The *Art Nouveau* mood is seen in the rose window on the south side of the tower and in the arches of the nave and rood beam carved with square panels of floral decoration. Much of this furniture and decorative detail was carried out by the Bromsgrove Guild. The furniture makes use of vari-coloured woods and recent panelling by Pancheri on the east wall has continued this theme. Altogether this is a most creditable piece of early twentieth-century craftsmanship and arouses a fresh interest in *Art Nouveau*, which is another example of a generation taking a more appreciative view of the tastes of its predecessor. An architect once remarked to us, 'I spent a good deal of my early career in destroying *Art Nouveau*.'

At Dodford was the site of one of Feargus O'Connor's 'National Land Scheme' projects of 1847; but like the rest it did not last long.

This is perhaps the place in which to insert a note about the Bromsgrove Guild which followed in the wake of Morris and the Arts and Crafts Movement at the beginning of this century. The firm of Pancheri which now carries on its traditions and its business continues to supply the churches of Worcestershire with beautiful things.

Chaddesley Corbett church has been described as the best example of fourteenth-century work in the County. It is unique, at any rate in one respect, for it is the only church in England dedicated in honour of St. Cassian who, in Butler's *Lives of the Saints*, is presented as a Christian schoolmaster at Imola who was condemned to death by his own scholars. It is comforting to know that our own contemporary 'blackboard jungle' has not gone quite so far as this. The church has a complicated architectural history beginning with extensive Norman remains and going on through its conspicuous fourteenth-century work to the late Perpendicular windows of the south aisle. But the *pièce de résistance* here is the font, twelfth century, and again affiliated to the Herefordshire school of carvers. It is profusely decorated and almost Kilpeck in sentiment with four dragons and inter-twisted tails. A fragment of a tympanum of Christ in Majesty in the porch is of much the same date as the font.

The village street will attract those who are not interested in churches. It has a fine array of timbered houses and, as a street, is conspicuous in its beauty in a country of beautiful villages. The Talbot Inn is perhaps the most obvious building but the Georgian houses also deserve careful notice.

So, at last, as a triumphant climax to this chapter we come to Harvington. Here we have, miraculously preserved for us, all that we so cruelly lost when Hindlip was filched from us by its Regency destroyers.

Harvington Hall was a Pakington house, acquired by Humphrey in 1529 but much altered by his son John between 1560 and 1575. The plan of the medieval house is traceable with its hall and solar and kitchen wings, but what we see is entirely Elizabethan. It stands, romantically, on a triangular site surrounded by a moat which broadens out into a pool on the north. There seem to have been swings of ecclesiastical allegiance in the Pakington family and in the seventeenth century John Pakington, his son Humphrey and Lady Mary Yate his grand-daughter were Roman Catholics and it must have been they who in that century created the priest-holes which are the most fascinating feature of the house. Probably it contains more of them, ingeniously contrived, than any other house in England. They were obviously needed, for the penal laws against Roman Catholics, which were initiated in Elizabethan times, went on fiercely into the following century and it was not far away from Harvington, at Rushock Court, that the Franciscan John Wall was arrested in 1679. He had celebrated mass at Harvington and had no doubt made use of the hiding places there. He was tried and condemned and executed at Worcester and was the last Roman Catholic priest to die for his faith in England. These fascinating priests' holes are freely shown to visitors for the house is now primarily a show place which is rightly and properly in the ownership of the Roman Catholic Arch Diocese of Birmingham. The holes are not the only striking feature of the place. The wall paintings of the Nine Worthies, of David slaying Goliath and the arabesques and floral patterns, and the strings of drops of blood which might have been a reminder of the Saviour's passion or of the possible fate of stubborn recusant priests in a room that must have been a chapel are a priceless survival of some of the decorative notions of our ancestors. Such wall paintings are scarce in the County though Dowles Manor, near Bewdley, has them on a smaller scale.

But we have branched off our main north-eastern spoke here to visit these three last places and Harvington has brought us pretty close to Kidderminster. That important manufacturing town and some other villages round it must wait until we make our last journey along the northern spoke to the northern fringe of the County.

CHAPTER SIX

North with the Severn

Our next journey from Worcester is along a northern spoke following the line of the Severn, and to reach this we cross the Worcester bridge and turn right along the west bank of the river until we reach the village of Hallow. Suburban building now stretches all the way and Hallow is a suburban village, but it still retains its individuality with an attractive village green on which children's festivities take place at appropriate times and which is surrounded by some pretty houses. Hallow church is big and impressive and shows what the Victorian builders could do in the way of Gothic when they had plenty of money behind them. There was certainly no stint here when W. J. Hopkins was given full rein in 1867. It is an opulent church in the style of 1300 with a tall broach spire and plentiful carved detail within. The reredos is something of a *tour de force* with its extremely realistic stone carved Calvary group by R. Boulton of Cheltenham. Though perhaps a trifle theatrical for some tastes it undoubtedly makes a memorable impact on most people who visit the church.

Further on we meet Grimley and Holt, two more riverside parishes. Before we get to Grimley church we may catch a glimpse on the left-hand side of the road across its fine parkland of the mansion called Thorngrove. This is an early nineteenth-century house in the classical mode, undistinguished architecturally except for its huge drawing room which housed to perfection the splendid collection of pictures assembled by its former owner, the late Col. Davison. But most people know Thorngrove because it was the temporary exile home of Lucien Bonaparte, Napoleon's brother. Grimley church, whose lineage is Norman and Early English has been much over-restored but at Holt we have one of the best-preserved of our Norman churches in the County. The detailed Norman work is plain to see; a south doorway, its pillars heavily ornamented by grotesque carving, the north doorway simpler but also with animal carving. The north windows of the nave are magnificent Norman work and there is everywhere a proliferation of zigzag mouldings and scalloped capitals. The chancel arch is a triumph of architectural preservation with a moulding of chain links and a beast's head at the apex. One is tempted to see the influence of the greatest of the Herefordshire school of carvers, as at Kilpeck or the Shobdon arches, but some experts are reluctant to admit any connection. There is a fine Norman font, drum-shaped and with monster heads and trailing tails surrounding the bowl. For the Norman enthusiast this is a most rewarding building.

But there are one or two surprises. Who would have expected a copy of a mosaic from the Mausoleum of Galla Placidia at Ravenna to have found its way above a Norman chancel arch in a Worcestershire country church; and this superb original Norman carving must have stimulated a lady 700 years later to see what she could do in the same line. The pulpit and lectern, which date from 1858, are in the Norman style and the work of none other than the wife of the vicar of the time. They will deceive no one of course, but the products of this formidable lady are worthy rather of respect than derision. There is a good tomb chest, nicely coloured, bearing the effigy of a lady, probably one of the Beauchamps and dating from the fifteenth century, among other monuments in the church.

Across the lane from the church is Holt Castle, a Beauchamp stronghold, reminding us of the period when the line of the Severn had to be defended against the marauding Welsh. It has a fourteenth-century tower, reminiscent of the peel towers which are so plentiful along the Scottish border. Additional accommodation was added in the early eighteenth century to supplement what remained of the medieval living rooms and there is a handsome staircase of that period and some interesting stucco work in the ceiling. The fifteenth-century hall, which survives, is enormous and provides excellent space for the meetings of local community groups whom the kindly owner allows to use it.

At the Lenchford Hotel, a little further down the river, a delightful

Lido has been developed in recent years. The enterprising proprietor has much expanded his business by exploiting the sailing facilities at this point and it is an enjoyable experience in warm summer months to sit in the hotel gardens and to watch the yachts with full bellying sails gliding to and fro along this stretch of water.

The next parish along the river is Shrawley, which again possesses a fine Norman church with much decorative detail. The west tower is seventeenth-century work and the nave has windows of about 1800. On the frontier of the parish with Astley, it is worth visiting an ecclesiastical establishment such as is rare in the Church of England. A little before the Glasshampton bridge which crosses the Dick brook a rough-surfaced track leads uphill to what is now generally known as Glasshampton Monastery. This has been fashioned from the stable block of the great eighteenth-century house of the Cookes family which was so completely destroyed by fire in 1810 that there is even some doubt as to precisely where the mansion stood. But there is no mistaking the stable block.

In 1918 Fr. William Sirr of the Community of the Divine Compassion, anxious to found a Contemplative Order within the Church of England was enabled with considerable local support to obtain possession of this stable block which, though dilapidated, was sturdily built and obviously possessed the sort of possibilities for the kind of settlement which Fr. William envisaged. The whole story of his life and of the Glasshampton enterprise has been told by Fr. Geoffrey Curtis, C.R. in his *William of Glasshampton, Friar, Monk, Solitary*. It is a story of glorious and sanctified failure. Fr. William never succeeded in gathering round him a band of like-minded aspirants who could accept the stern discipline of the contemplative life. But the influence which he had both upon earnest seekers after the truth and the vagrants and social casualties who sought him out and found temporary sanctuary there was quite incalculable. When Fr. William died in 1939 it could be said that apart from friends who visited him, he died truly a solitary, alone. He is buried there in the cloister garth.

When the writer first visited the place in 1945 it was neglected, dusty, unkempt, but not derelict. It had done service in housing war refugees but the question then was, what possible use could the

Church of England make of it? Then, providentially, a use was found. The Society of St. Francis, a popular Anglican order with its headquarters at Cerne Abbas in Dorset, was able to utilize it as a home for its novitiate. So now the vision of Fr. William has been realised, though in a somewhat more active idiom, and the old stable block with its pyramidal angle turrets and its centre with pediment and lantern is a place of adventure for young men who are pledged to a life offered to the Franciscan ideal, as well as to local clergymen and others who visit it for quiet and rest and the replenishment of spiritual springs. Those who knew him are sure that Fr. William would have been well satisfied.

We cross the Glasshampton bridge into the parish of Astley; and here await us personal associations of equal interest though vastly different kind. From the monastic solitary we turn to one of the most significant figures in the recent political history of England. For here, at Astley Hall, was the home of Stanley Baldwin, Prime Minister. In the mid-1940s, when the writer had the privilege of some small acquaintance with Lord Baldwin, the ex-Premier was drawing near the end of his life which had reached a somewhat sad and lonely phase. Lonely is perhaps too astringent a word, for his friends and neighbours remained loyal to him and he was seen at local functions such as speech days at Hartlebury Grammar School. Baldwin was a most loyal and enthusiastic son of Worcestershire. Born at Bewdley he retained an intense love of his County and it would probably be true to say that he was never really happy away from it. He was a considerable classical scholar and perhaps he would have been happier had he remained all his life a cultured country squire. But a series of improbable political manoeuvres set him in the highest political office. He retired in some honour and lustre for his deft handling of the General Strike and the Abdication Crisis. But when war came in 1939 his public image radically changed. Some sections of the public were delighted to find a scapegoat for the disaster; he was the recipient of anonymous letters in great quantity, vilifying him for his supposed responsibility for the war, and there was that malevolent incident of the forcible removal of those handsome memorial gates which were considered an essential contribution to the sinews of war. It is interesting to note that his most recent

biographers seem inclined somewhat to redress the unfavourable balance. Faults of unpreparedness there undoubtedly were, but it is at least understandable that this traditional Christian Englishman found it hard to appreciate that such powers of wickedness were arising on the Continent, nor was it easy to provide adequate defensive measures in a climate of thought so intensely pacific as that represented by the League of Nations Peace Referendum.

When in 1946 the writer had the great privilege of a long and wide-ranging conversation with the Elder Statesman he found him, though painfully crippled by an arthritic complaint, extremely acute in mind and very ready to converse upon contemporary persons and events. (Re Winston Churchill: '*In the 1930s his stock was at very bottom. He was the most miserable and disgruntled man in the House of Commons, yet he had planned and trained himself for a lifetime to be a great war Prime Minister. I congratulated him that his success and popularity had not turned his head. Churchill said "At any rate you know that I am not conceited". He uses words very carefully.*' Re King Edward VIII: '*I knew him very well and I think he was fond of me; Mrs. Simpson has probably by this time cured him of that.*')

Two recollections remain particularly of that encounter. One is of the multitude of pipes which occupied ledges and bowls around the room. Baldwin's pipe was a gift to the cartoonists of the time; a feature in which he has been imitated by a later day Prime Minister of a different political persuasion. The second is of the rare courtesy with which, though his painful complaint made walking difficult, he conducted this stranger visitor to his front door and graciously bade him a friendly farewell.

The Hall is now a home for underprivileged children from Birmingham. Near by is Astley church where Baldwin found spiritual comfort in the last days of his life in acts of frequent Holy Communion. Though his forebears were Methodists he had been throughout his life a conforming Churchman, following his father Alfred Baldwin, the local industrialist, who had joined the Church of England. But his mother had been one of the four remarkable Macdonald sisters, daughters of a Methodist minister. One had married Alfred Baldwin, another Sir Edward Burne-Jones, another Sir Edward Poynter, President of the Royal Academy and another was the mother of Rudyard Kipling. Baldwin had taken his ecclesiastical duties with much seriousness. He spoke with great reverence and respect of Randall Davidson. He was not particularly familiar with William Temple, but said that he had greatly appreciated a letter of sympathy which Temple had written from Hartlebury when he was in one of the troughs of political depression. He was proud of his appointment of Bishop White-Thompson as Bishop of Ely for he was anxious to find a man who he was sure would be a spiritual father to the lonely fen priests. He had a great respect for Hensley Henson, whom he regarded as a man of outstanding ability who would have gone to the top in whatever profession he had chosen. Baldwin relied much on Archdeacon Vernon Storr for suggestions as to prospective bishops from the Evangelical party. It was not easy to find suitable candidates from this party, later in his reign; 'we had used them all up.' He tried to keep a fair balance of ecclesiastical parties in his appointments.

So, at the altar rail of this, one of the finest of the Norman churches in our County, the former maker of Bishops and leader of the country over one of its stormiest and most critical constitutional epochs, made his final peace with God. Here he knelt in a church lavishly built about 1160, rich with Norman detail and hard by the Elizabethan tombs of the Blount family, great ones of the earth in times which must have seemed equally troublous to his own world of General Strike and Abdication and Global War. May his memory be honoured for he was, according to the lights of his Worcestershire mind and upbringing, an honest man.

When the traveller crosses the parish boundary at Astley Cross into Areley Kings he is in what to the present writer is veritably hallowed ground. For it was here that in 1944, a little before D-day, he first encountered Worcestershire. Arriving hot foot from the rather dreary back streets—now long demolished—of a Lancashire cotton town and alighting upon this beautiful hill overlooking the Severn and crowned with Norman church, Queen Anne Rectory and half-timbered buildings, could he, in that honeymoon interlude which included VE day and VJ day, have been much blamed for thinking that he had arrived in Paradise? Nor is he altogether wrong in describing it as hallowed ground; for, popularly, at one time, it was known as 'the Christian Shore'. On the opposite bank of the Severn there was no place of worship between the river and Kidderminster until the simple brick building of Mitton Chapel was erected on the far edge of what is now Stourport in 1782.

But on the west bank and in part of the wide-spreading manor of Martley and hard by the Manor house itself, there had existed a church since Norman times. The Manor, at various times, was a royal possession and this part bore the name which connects it with the King. The connection was further sustained by the fact that from earliest times the Rector of Martley has appointed the Rector of Areley Kings. And this has resulted in an extraordinarily interesting family complex whereby for 300 years two notable families, the Vernons and the Hastings, have occupied these two benefices as 'squarsons'. The normal pattern was that father occupied the parent living at Martley ('one of the most valuable in the County, especially in a good year of hops') while son subsisted on a much more modest endowment at Areley Kings. Upon papa's sad demise, son sailed triumphantly into the parent living and the enjoyment of a much more considerable income. This pattern continued with a minor interruption, from the Restoration until 1958 when the writer, though not of the family, succeeded the last of the Hastings. At his retirement in 1972 diocesan authority decided to sell the ancient Martley Rectory with its too extensive grounds, so the present writer sadly withdraws into the shadows consoling himself with the doubtful distinction of being 'the last of the squarsons'.

But the rectors of Areley Kings number a much more notable priest than those on their roll—none other than Layamon, the author of *Brut* who informs us at the beginning of his long epic poem that 'there was a priest in the land who was named Layamon: he was son of Leovenath. . . . He dwelt at "Earnley", at a noble church upon Severns bank—good it seemed to him—near Redstone, where he read book', which is to say that there he said mass. It has been suggested that he may have occupied one of the cave dwellings which honeycombed the red rocks on the river's edge. However that may be, he left us the curious poem, a metrical and entirely mythical account of the origins of the British race, which may still be seen in the British Museum. What is more important than the subject matter of the poem is the fact that writing about 1200 he is evocative of a period when the racial strains were mingling into a common British stock with the antipathies formerly associated with those strains now forgotten in an emerging new nationhood.

There is a curious early reminiscence of Layamon in the church, apart from the little stained glass portrait which fills a small Norman window on the south side of the sanctuary. The modern font is placed on a Norman base and that base is incised with lettering, admittedly of later date, which reads 'TEMPORE LA AMANNI SANTI'. The original font without doubt would be of Layamon's time, but what later hand has proclaimed him 'saint'? Certainly no formal process of canonisation has set him in glory; here surely is one of those 'saints of popular acclaim' whom local sentiment insisted upon honouring. Perhaps as a symbol of that peaceful mingling of the racial strains he deserves a mead of beatific appreciation. We will not grudge it him.

This church of St. Bartholomew, Areley Kings, retains its small Norman chancel and its tower beneath which is the main entrance to the church, its lower stage Decorated, its upper stage, Perpendicular. But that is all that is old; the nave and north aisle were rebuilt by Preedy in 1885, an operation which caused a painful rift in the squarsonical family. But it is a very pleasant piece of work; clean and light and airy and filled by the present incumbent with many beautiful things, this church in the estimation of the present writer is one of the most satisfying ecclesiastical buildings in the County.

There are other things at Areley Kings which the visitor must not miss. The lovely wisteria- and magnolia-clad rectory is a Jacobean house, much altered in the 1730s; there is a curious horizontal in-filling between the pointed gables designed by the Georgian restorers to strike a contemporary classical note. They also provided an exquisite staircase and panelling within. At the bottom of the garden stands a curious gazebo or garden house built at the time of the restoration: Richard Vernon designated it, in a Latin inscription, 'a retreat from domestic cares'. A Victorian rector furnished its upper floor with bookshelves to do duty as 'an outside study': his children pounced on the phrase, conveniently shortening it to the name which it bore ever afterwards—'the outstout'. At the churchyard gate stands a half-timbered building of fifteenth-century construction; historians differ as to whether it is the pre-Reformation rectory or the Church House where in pre-Puritan times the Church ales were brewed and parochial functions held. In the churchyard is a short length of stone, at one time part of the boundary fence. It is inscribed: 'LITHOLOGEMA QUARE: REPONITUR SIR HARRY.' This curious jumble of Greek, Latin and English means 'Why a stone monument? Sir Harry lies here'. It is the grave of Sir Harry Coningsby, who in extremes of grief at the end of the seventeenth century retired to live at a small property, the Sturt, which he owned in the parish after accidentally dropping his only child into the moat at his home at Weld Hall, Shenley, Hertfordshire where the child was drowned. He planted three walnut trees near the wall and made a bequest that the boys of the parish were to crack nuts on his monument on a certain day in the year. The original trees eventually died, but in 1948 the excellent rector planted three more in pious hope that present-day choir boys might in due course be able to implement Sir Harry's original intention.

Areley Hall, an imposing half-timbered mansion of about 1500, stands at the foot of the hill near the river bank. It was very much altered in Victorian times, but in spite of the way in which the rooms have been pulled about it is still possible to trace the usual pattern of medieval domestic building in the house. Happily it still remains the delightful home of the descendants of the people who built it; by female descent it has come down from Mucklow to Zachary and from Zachary to its present owners, the Lloyd family. It was the manor house of the wide spreading parish of Martley and in earliest times the adjacent church was probably built as a chapel of ease for the Hall family, who lived so far away from their parish church. Near by is Areley House, built in the eighteenth century when the Zachary family preferred the new look of Georgian mansion to their half-timbered ancestral home. The County now administers it as an Old People's Home.

When we came to live at Areley Kings in 1944 we estimated the population of what was then an entirely rural parish at about 900 people. By 1947 when we left, with memories of the lads of the village letting off rockets from the church tower on VE day and of a world trying slowly to adjust itself to peaceful conditions after six years of war, radical changes were taking place. The Stourport U.D.C. had bought land extensively in the parish and as we looked back wistfully over our shoulders in farewell, the first tenants were arriving to occupy the first houses on the Walshes Estate. Now Areley Kings is 'Stourport-over-the-River' with a population that cannot be much less than 7,000. But mercifully the little enclave of historic tradition on the hill top still survives unimpaired, though a great tide of villa building has swept up to it and surrounded it.

So, leaving Areley House on our left and crossing the bridge, we arrive in Georgian Town, Stourport-on-Severn. It is a curious fact that Stourport should be the only town in the County which grew up as a result of the canal system. It is a mushroom growth but a mushroom with a peculiarly delightful Georgian flavour. When Bewdley in 1776 declined to tolerate Brindley's 'stinking ditch' to join the waters of Severn and Trent, Stourport showed greater foresight by accepting a waterway to join Severn and Stour. Its reward was an immediate accession of trade and the appearance of the handsome boom town. As we cross the bridge, made of iron and built in 1870, we notice how well in recent years Stourport has managed its river. The banks are pleasantly laid out and there are the usual tourist amenities, which in high summer make the town a kind of Midland Blackpool. But over the bridge we are at once in the nucleus of the Georgian town, a shining example of the way in which the late eighteenth-century people could create a beautiful townscape with their façades of thinly sashed windows and pedimented porticos. There is nothing much more to invite the visitor to do than to walk around Lichfield Street, and Bridge Street and New Street so as to note these details. An architectural student with his pencil and notebook could spend a very profitable afternoon's perambulation in this way.

The church at the top of the town has a curious history. The first chapelry of Mitton, as it was then called, was taken out of the parish of Kidderminster in 1782 as we should quite expect; it was a plain uninspiring specimen of that period built in brick. Then, in 1881, a church designed by Sir Gilbert Scott in his grand manner was begun to fit the matured dignity of the new town. It was a big church, almost cathedral-like, but unfortunately it was never finished. A quarrel between Mr. John Brinton of Moor Hall, the local rich man, and the Revd. Benjamin Gibbons the vicar, also rich, brought the excellent work to a standstill. So there is a large nave, but no chancel and no tower and spire as was originally intended, and even in the nave uncut stone betrays the unfinished details. A recent enterprise in finishing off the west end with monies accumulated over the years in a vain effort to complete the church according to its original plan does not strike one as particularly successful.

Of course the town grew even after the canal era had run its short-lived course. The canal basin affords exciting exploration for industrial archaeology and the curious may speculate how the Tontine Inn of 1788, here, comes to be so named. Modern industry has invaded the town with Parsons Chain Company, the Steatite works and the huge Power Station, of 1925, 1936 and 1946. The latest evidence of municipal enterprise is a Civic Centre built at the end of Georgian New Street in 1963. Now we are told that this forward-looking building is too constricted for the future local government of the area and that a new and larger centre of civil administration must be built elsewhere. Stourport is a tidy, compact and well-governed town; it is spreading hugely in the direction of Bewdley and it will be interesting in the near future to see whether it can continue to preserve its cherished independence of Kidderminster.

We are very close to Kidderminster here, but it may at this point be more convenient to take the road to the south-east and go and look at Hartlebury. As we climb the hill road out of the town in that direction let us turn to the left along Wilden Lane and explore that village. Here was the foundation of the iron fortune of the Baldwin family, a part of which was surrendered to the State by Stanley Baldwin as a contribution to the extinguishing of the National Debt, a suggestion made *pour encourager les autres* in a famous letter to *The Times* under the initials F.S.T. We have never heard that 'the others' responded with much alacrity. But the object of our journey here is Wilden church built in 1880 by Alfred Baldwin at the design of W. J. Hopkins and testifying both to the enthusiasm of his Anglicanism and the usefulness of his family connections. The church is nothing much, but go inside and you stand inside a veritable jewelled lantern. This time it is not amid the exquisite colouring of fifteenth-century Malvern glass, but in the loveliness of Morris's windows, designed by Burne-Jones. They are all of a piece and probably unique because of that. We talk much of the loss of the art of stained-glass making after the Reformation, but there is plenty of evidence here that by the end of the nineteenth century the Pre-Raphaelites and their followers had gone pretty far in recovering it.

So continue up the main road of the hill from Stourport, drop down on the other side and you are in Hartlebury. There are four things we shall mention here in this well-known place. It is worth looking at the church, especially if you are interested in the revived Gothic of the early nineteenth century, for it is by Rickman, one of the earliest practitioners of that art. Although scarcely as successful as his Ombersley, it has a certain elegance with its thin Perpendicular piers and its plaster vaults with ridge ribs. The tower dates from 1587 when it was built for Bishop Sandys, the north chancel chapel from about 1300, and the Rickman work is 1825 and 1836.

Hartlebury Rectory is a joy; built in that Queen Anne period which is probably the acme of all English domestic building. The exquisite balance of the sash-windowed façade and the lovely scallop-shell porch canopy give some excuse to those who have believed that it is a Wren house. Unfortunately there is no evidence that Wren built either this or any other parsonage house and although he was a friend of Bishop Stillingfleet and stayed at the Castle and although James Stillingfleet, the Bishop's son, built the house we cannot say more than that James may have hearkened to the great architect's advice and that the house is of 'the school of Wren'.

The village possesses an ancient Grammar School, housed in new buildings which have been partially rebuilt after a recent fire. It was refounded at the initiative of Bishop Sandys in 1558 and among the foundation statutes is the engaging provision that 'the school-master and usher shall and may have use and take the profits of all such cockfights and potations as be commonly used in schools'. Contemporary schoolboy vices are hardly likely to be so profitable to the authorities.

But it is the Castle which most visitors come to Hartlebury to see, and since the Episcopate has lately entered the Stately Homes business there is no reason why you should not now turn the nose of your car into the long tree-lined drive which leaves the Stourport road a little outside the village. Lest the modern conscience should be troubled at the notion of a twentieth-century Bishop living in a Castle, we must discharge all scruples by explaining at the start that the left wing with its modest suite of rooms and its 'Strawberry Hill Gothick' chapel remodelled for Bishop Maddox in the middle of the eighteenth century are all that the present-day Bishop has been allowed personally to retain of the former episcopal splendour.

The centre block contains the fifteenth-century great hall and the 1760 saloon and the right-hand side is the headquarters of the excellent County Museum the nucleus of the contents of which is the remarkable collection of local memorabilia bequeathed to the County by the late Mr. J. F. Parker who built it up over many years at his home at Tickenhill Palace, Bewdley. The original castle was, of course, a fortified stronghold, first built by Bishop Walter de Cantelupe about 1255 and Bishop Giffard who finished it in 1268. But the medieval castle was largely destroyed in 1646 during the Civil War and rebuilt between the end of the seventeenth and the end of the eighteenth centuries. So what we really see is a widespreading and spacious country house mostly of Georgian atmosphere. The porch, bearing the coloured arms of Bishop Fleetwood who built it, comes from 1680. The Great Hall has pseudo-Gothic pointed windows and glazing bars of the late eighteenth century and a very high roof with thin timbers and wall posts. This hall is arrayed with a whole series of portraits of Bishops of Worcester from Reformation times. Mrs. Charles-Edwards, wife of a former Bishop, took much interest in these portraits and attached explanatory labels to each so that what you see is a complete and useful symposium of the Worcester episcopate. The other apartment at the south end of the hall is the Saloon with delightful flimsy Rococo ceiling and wall decoration of 1760. The Great Hall and Saloon are in constant public use for ecclesiastical and County gatherings, so democratic sentiment is entirely satisfied. Up the staircase of 1680 is the Hurd library of the late eighteenth century in the Adam idiom, with delicate plaster work and handsome bookcases housing the library which that most cultured and erudite of Augustan Bishops bequeathed to the See.

How often when the agenda of Rural Deans' meetings has seemed tedious and overlong has the writer consoled his soul by drinking in the loveliness of the Rococo swirling arabesques in the Saloon or the beauty of the plaster work and the cases filled with calf-bound, gilt-tooled folios in the Hurd library! Bishops, agendas and beauty; these three and the greatest of these is beauty.

We return to Stourport in order to reach Bewdley. If we take the road along the east bank we pass through the quickly spreading suburbs of the town, which look as though they are stretching out in a desperate effort to race us to Bewdley and pass through Wribbenhall before we reach the town. Here is a church by Arthur Blomfield built in 1878 in the style of 1300, and the mansion and park of Spring Grove, formerly the seat of the well-known Webb family but now undergone a strange transmogrification into a safari park of wild life. Along this route also is evidence of cave dwellings and a Hermitage in the Blackstone Rock. On the other side of the river the road to Bewdley passes at the foot of the hill on which Areley Kings church stands, traversing some spectacular river scenery and entering the town via the more ancient neighbourhood of Ribbesford.

Here the church is of considerable interest, particularly because of its south arcade which comes from the fifteenth century and is the only example of a timber arcade of pillars in the County. But the church is of Norman origin and there is Norman masonry in the south aisle and some curious carvings and mouldings. The tympanum with its archer and two quadrupeds is a notable feature. Much of the church was rebuilt in 1877 somewhat, we are told by Pevsner, to Ruskin's displeasure. There is stained glass in the west window designed by Burne-Jones, made by Morris and Co. in 1875 and given, quite as we should expect, by Alfred Baldwin. Ribbesford House, large and impressive, is a trifle disappointing. It was certainly there in 1535, but it has been drastically altered and restored. Its last claim to fame is that it was the headquarters of the Free French Forces during the Second World War.

Bewdley brings us nearly to the end of this spoke of our wheel and it is not at all a bad climax to our present exploration; for Bewdley is and always has been a place of some consequence, though its name has probably become more widely known to the general public since an ennobled Prime Minister incorporated the name of his birthplace in his title. Bewdley's era of greatest prosperity was when the Severn was the great highway of commerce bringing the world's merchandise through the port of Bristol and distributing it far into the English Midlands. Its rise and decline and hence its present architectural configuration is very much the same as that of Upton. A good example of the commercial prosperity of Bewdley is to be found in the Prattinton family, long connected with the grocery trade, who had always done considerable business with Bristol merchants barge trading to Bewdley and to the other Severn depots: Peter Prattinton himself writes: 'The Bewdley grocers have been a flourishing set of People. They have carried on a very extensive Wholesale Trade in furnishing the inland Shops of the County round them with such commodities as Bristol could supply them with.' It was the family fortune thus built up which enabled Peter Prattinton, who graduated as Bachelor of Medicine in 1797, to decline a medical career and upon the death of his father to apply his unceasing energy to the pursuit of Worcestershire history and antiquities. He was no doubt wise to relinquish family trade at that time for Bewdley's categorical refusal of Brindley's canal had hastened its own decline in favour of boom-town Stourport; in any event the coming of railways inevitably meant the decline of both towns. However, Bewdley is proud of its traditions as a considerable inland port and the aldermen of its council used to wear blue robes in recognition of this marine connection.

While referring to Bewdley's trade it would be a pity to omit a mention of its important horn industry, which flourished until the beginning of this century in the manufacture of horn drinking cups, lanterns, combs, snuff boxes and similar articles.

There was also an active trade in the manufacture of caps, and people of the district were compelled to wear one on pain of a fine of 3s. 4d.

But all this trade and industry was a secondary thing to Bewdley's aristocratic past. Licensed for a market under Richard, Duke of York in 1446 and incorporated under Edward IV, the ancient seat of the Mortimers at Tickenhill served for a while as a royal palace. Early in the sixteenth century it became the seat of the Council of the Marches of Wales and here in 1501 Prince Arthur, eldest son of Henry VII, was betrothed to Katherine of Aragon and married by proxy. Here his body rested on the way from Ludlow Castle, where he died, to Worcester Cathedral where he was buried. Tickenhill Palace or Manor is now largely a 1740 building, but it contains roof timbers of the fifteenth century hall which preceded it. Many of us were grateful, some 30 years ago, for the never-failing hospitality of the late Mr. J. F. Parker and his wife who lived in the house and were invariably prepared to display the treasures of their own private Folk Museum which are now at Hartlebury Castle.

Leland praised the town greatly in 1540. The church at the centre, St. Anne, was originally a chantry chapel and in the middle of the fifteenth century it became a chapelry of Ribbesford. The west tower dates from 1695 and the rest of the church from 1745 when its architect was Thomas Woodward of Chipping Campden. It is on an island site and traffic swirls around it. The main street is Load Street which runs from the church to the bridge, a beautiful structure built by Telford in 1795. Load Street, Severnside and High Street contain outstanding houses, hotels and public buildings of every period and style, half-timbered, Georgian, Victorian. They are excellently catalogued in Pevsner's guide where it is praised as the most perfect Georgian town in Worcestershire, which must be preserved at all costs. There is an active Civic Society at work here which by its constant vigilance is likely to see that this is done.

The diligent may discover in High Street the sturdy Georgian house now marked by a tablet, where a Prime Minister of England was born, and there are architectural delights at every turn. A little outside the town is Dowles Manor, which should certainly be visited if opportunity allows, for not only is it an exceptionally complete small Elizabethan Manor house but it contains some of the most perfect wall decorations of its period in existence. In grey and red there are stylized arabesques and even an Elizabethan lady and gentleman, a pleasing costume study of the times.

Further up the river is Upper Arley and after that the Severn leaves Worcestershire for Shropshire. It was here, in 'a true arcardian villa', that the 'bad' Lord Lyttelton's sister Lucy and her husband, Lord Valentia, later Lord Mountnorris, with their children, found some happiness in the 1770s. The story of the ill-starred brother and sister and a fairer appraisal of the former's character is finely told in Reginald Blunt's *Thomas, Lord Lyttelton*. There was once a Norman church, but the present building is of the early fourteenth century with much subsequent rebuilding. There is a good east window by Kempe of 1887 and a cross-legged knight of the early fourteenth century. Once there was an Arley Castle, but that was largely early Victorian, built by Lord Mountnorris in 1844, and it has recently been demolished.

The Severn now flows on towards Shrewsbury and for many years you might have accompanied it on the train along what was known as the Severn Valley Line, surely one of the most picturesque branch lines in the country. Then the 'Beeching axe' closed the line as uneconomical. This chapter may well close with the cheerful note that it has recently been re-opened as a private venture and the hard physical labour which has been put into its resurrection cannot be overpraised. It deserves, and has received, much influential support.

CHAPTER SEVEN

Towards the Northern Border

We have travelled to the rim of our County wheel in every direction but one; there remains the spoke which takes us direct north to what some would call the industrial fringe. But, in truth, that industrial area is, as far as Worcestershire is concerned, such a small eastern area of our northern frontier that it is better to say that we are travelling north in order to explore the northern frontier as a whole. Certainly we shall meet some large towns where industry has long had a grip, Kidderminster, Stourbridge, Halesowen, Dudley, and if we retain the Poet Laureate's pleasing image of the burnt pie crust we shall find in fact, that a burnt bit of the crust has detached itself and become entirely surrounded by Staffordshire. But the grimy industrialism of these towns is a small price to pay for some of the glorious country which stretches even across the northern border from the Lickey and Clent Hills to the upper reaches of the Worcestershire Teme and the cider orchards of Tenbury.

We leave Worcester City by the direct northern route, taking the left-hand road at Barbourne which we declined when we followed the north-easternly fork to Droitwich. It is a short journey to one of our show villages, Ombersley, grouped around a crossroads. This is a busy junction if ever there was one, with the right-hand road going east until it meets the long wall behind which lies the Westwood we have already visited and then on to Droitwich, and the left-hand road making for Holt Fleet where Telford's iron one-arched bridge of 1828 spans the Severn. Then that road goes on to Holt Heath and Great Witley. Some motorists have been found who considered it worthwhile to come back north as far as Holt bridge rather than waste their time in an attempt to cross the Severn at the heavily congested Worcester bridge. Busy indeed is the main street that is Ombersley with its crossroads, and something of an adventure even to cross this so-called village street; but that may soon be a thing of the past for we have been promised, in the very near future, another motor road which will by-pass Ombersley to the east and then we shall be able properly to appreciate the beauties of this village without danger to life and limb.

Beauties there certainly are in abundance, for here is one of the best collection of timbered houses in the County. Stroll hither and thither, keeping that wary eye alert for the main-road traffic and look at the ancient houses, the pubs, the Crown and Sandys and the King's Arms, at the Dower House near the roundabout and a few Georgian houses in brick including the vicarage, a late eighteenth-century house. This has indeed everything that a picture-book village ought to have, with a fine commanding church at the centre and the squire's mansion a little to the south. This is well seen from the main road, a neo-classical house, recreated in stone by J. Webb in 1812. The principal entrance on the east is by a porch with Ionic columns. The lofty entrance hall is two-storied with fine ceiling, pilasters and niches. The principal rooms are panelled in dark wood, the saloon has its marble chimney-piece and the staircase and its plaster ceiling are part of the original house before Webb began his re-making and date from 1725. Upstairs there is a room with painted Chinese silk panels and door curtains which may remind you of the Regent's Brighton Pavilion. This is a house of much dignity and culture and the home of Lord and Lady Sandys, whose family have touched the civil and ecclesiastical life of Worcestershire for some hundreds of years at many points. The joyful thing here is that Ombersley Court is a home, restored and rehabilitated by a young couple who, on inheriting it, were determined to make the place the best that it possibly could be made. There seems to be a lesson here, that many more of these great and precious houses could have been saved as homes if their owners had had the wisdom and the careful financial strategy and above all the unflinching will and determination to preserve them. Often we feel that these irreplaceable monuments of beauty and tradition have been lost because their owners simply had not the will and therefore the 'know-how' to save the situation. We are grateful that this was not so at Ombersley.

The church is a remarkable period piece, the period being the earliest experimental phase of the nineteenth-century Gothic Revival. The architect is Rickman, who invented the classic nomenclature of the medieval Gothic styles, and the church dates from the late 1820s. How successful he was here as a beginner in the field, with his stately tower, his flying buttresses, his soaring roof and clever plaster rib vaults! True, some of these features may seem thin by the standards of later accomplished Gothic practitioners, but what a gallant bit of pioneering! We like a few of the less obvious details, too; the fireplace in the squire's pew, the way the galleries are set back a little from the arcades, the wondrous iron heating stove on the north wall; never must it be jettisoned. And while it is not possible to enthuse about the stained glass it is entirely congruous to its period and we can be relieved to know that the later Victorians had better things in store. But all in all, this is a valuable church, a significant landmark on the road to the recovery of the authentic English Gothic tradition as it was to be reinterpreted within the next 70 years by the greatest of the Victorian masters.

The Sandys Mausoleum is a fragment of medievalism on the same site. A little to the south of the present church it stands, its north and south walls of late thirteenth-century work, its east and west walls of 1830. Here are buried members of the family, but the wall tablets in the chancel of the church are worth reading carefully as a voluble symposium of Sandys family history.

Beyond Ombersley the main road continues, dead north, to Kidderminster, passing through Crossway Green, leaving Hartlebury a little to the west and Stourport-on-Severn beyond it. Between Ombersley and Crossway Green it passes through a plethora of Hamptons—Uphampton, Sytchhampton, Brookhampton, Comhampton, Dunhampton and even Northampton; how confusing can the map get? But on the east side of the road is the site of one of the several oak trees under which St. Augustine is supposed to have met the British bishops; hence confusion may be worse confounded. However, the site has been assured of its immortality by the naming of the adjacent hotel, the Mitre Oak. Doverdale, a tiny village with

28   (*opposite above*) *Harvington Hall* – '*headquarters of the Jesuit underground*'

29   (*below*) *Chaddesley Corbett from the Church Tower*

TO THE GLORY OF GOD AND IN LOVING
MEMORY OF ENOCH BALDWIN WHO DEPARTED
THIS LIFE JVNE 11 TH 1905 AGED 32 YEARS

a small church on the east of the road, is worth a glance. The church is of twelfth-century origin with some interesting glass and a fifteenth-century bell; it was much restored in 1833 and 1850. Doverdale Manor is an impressive Georgian house. Waresley, an outlying bit of Hartlebury is on the main road. The big house here was the home of the Revd. Benjamin Gibbons whose shade disconsolately haunts it in regret that he quarrelled with Mr. John Brinton and failed to complete his fine new Scott church at Stourport to which he commuted on Sundays. The phenomenon does not disturb the inhabitants, who are the boys of an Approved School which has its home there. So, leaving a widespread government depot on our left at Summerfield we reach a point where the great high-rising flats of the Council stretch up into the sky at Hoo Brook like fingers beckoning us into the town of Kidderminster.

Here indeed we encounter Worcester industrialism for the first time. Where factory walls line the streets we might think ourselves in a Lancashire town. But it is all on such a small scale, and a mile or two's journey in any direction from the town centre will take you in a few minutes back into delightful country. It is not a town of spectacular building achievement and indeed, at the present time, as with so many similar towns, it is busily engaged in sloughing off its old skin and assuming a new one, so that it is difficult to appraise justly what the new Kidderminster is likely to be. New trunk roads have rightly been one of its immediate concerns and it may be that the engineers have been right in their new arrangements. But one aspect, at least, terrified us. We used to like to walk up Church Street to view the fine parish church and reflect upon the delicious custom whereby the inhabitants of this street of 'peace and good neighbourhood' used, on Midsummer Eve, to settle their differences and quarrels and enjoy the bequest of the bachelor John Brecknell who left money to provide a twopenny plum cake, pipes, tobacco and ale for those who had so composed their differences. One would like to think that they then cemented their new peace and harmony by a visit to the parish church for some devotional exercise. But they and we would find it an almost suicidal gesture in these days, for the civic planners, in their wisdom, have struck the great new road across the top of Church Street and cut it off from the church. Now the new

30 (*opposite*) *Wilden – Burne-Jones and Morris*

ring road seems to have isolated this splendid church on a detached site. The removal of Richard Baxter (statue by Thomas Brock, 1875) from the Bull Ring and his re-positioning near the church was probably right. He raises a minatory finger to exhort the planners as he did on that 22 September 1642, when 'out of curiosity' he joined the crowds who had strolled out of Worcester to 'see the soldiers' and had preached a sermon to them. At least, he *would* have wagged that minatory finger today, but the last time we were there someone had broken it off and it was missing.

But these traffic hazards must not deter us from visiting St. Mary's, Kidderminster, for it is a grand church and though much restored and Victorianised it is entirely worthy to be the civic church of an important town. It is late medieval work. The massive fifteenth-century tower, the sixteenth-century aisles and arcades are all enormously Victorianised. We have always particularly enjoyed the rows of square-headed clerestory windows, the glass ornamented with all shapes of coloured angels. Then, the former Lady Chapel is a separate sixteenth-century building at the east end of the church which did service as King Charles' Grammar School after the King's charter to the town in 1636. The school stayed there until the middle of the last century when it moved to new premises on the Bewdley Road. There has been much refacing, restoration and enlargement over the centuries and the last handsome gift is the Whittall Chapel on the north-east side of the church, where an American donor substantially enriched the building in a gesture of gratitude to the territory of his ancestors. There are many treasures in this church; a superb brass, one of the finest in the County, to a lady and her two successive husbands, tomb chests and recumbent alabaster effigies to Cookeseys and Blounts and Beauchamps. There are wonderful displays of armour and costume in all these memorials.

Four other churches deserve mention. St. George's was a Commissioners type of church designed by Francis Goodwin in the 1820s; then in 1924 it was gutted by fire which gave Sir Giles Gilbert Scott the chance to come in and remake it. There is a remarkable combination of talent in the result; the east rose window with a great curtain sweeping up from the altar to meet it is particularly striking. St. John's looks like two churches side by side. The original was by

Alexander in 1843; then in 1890 Chatwin put a huge and lofty nave on the north side. Perhaps it was all cleverly done for so much of both buildings survived, but it resulted in an immensely large church. Very recently the church authorities have devised an ingenious new plan to economise space and heat: the arcades up to their tympana have been infilled so that the nave of Chatwin's church becomes the main worshipping space and the former side aisles are cut into ancillary rooms around it. This was regarded very much as a pilot scheme, for it was realised that other similar churches with over much space might adopt this same arrangement. It still remains to be seen whether St. John's has pioneered a really successful project which may well be followed elsewhere. Holy Innocents, Foley Park, built between the wars, is a spacious enterprise in a modern Byzantine idiom and St. Oswald's Broadwaters can be assigned to no tradition, the modern architect adventuring in making the most of his delightful watered site by producing a building with a hugely sloping roof in a style which we could only rather weakly dismiss by calling it 'contemporary'. It is not everyone's joy but it is a brave piece of work and well worth examination.

So much for ecclesiastical buildings; and what else of interest remains? A little industrial archaeology perhaps, if you like looking at old mills and forges. The name of the town inevitably suggests carpets and the first factory for this purpose was built in 1735; by 1772 there were 1700 silk and worsted looms at work. But this was only a new chapter in Kidderminster's industrial life for cloth had been woven there since the thirteenth century, and then had followed all sorts of refinements in the textile trade from Spanish poplins and arras to frieze and prunellas. The carpet manufacture was largely in the hands of family firms whose names, the Brintons, the Grosvenors, the Tomkinsons and many others have contributed much to the political and cultural life of the County. 'Carpet Trades', with which Sir Herbert Smith was associated, was an early amalgamation which may well set an economic pattern for the future. But at present, individualism seems to manage to survive and Kidderminster is a prosperous place.

Two great names are commemorated by statues. Richard Baxter on his newly sited perch has already been mentioned. His communion table is in the Chapel which bears his name and other bits and pieces which belonged to him may be found elsewhere in the town. Sir Rowland Hill, inventor of the Penny Post, is also delineated in a statue by Sir Thomas Brock outside the Town Hall; we have no means of knowing what he would have thought about present soaring postal rates. There are no particularly good civic buildings. So this is about all we can say concerning Kidderminster; the future for which it is so busily planning will no doubt have something good in store for it.

After Kidderminster our northern spoke must be sharply bent to the east and we will enjoy a brief pastoral interlude before we tackle our remaining industrial towns. There are a few country villages in the close neighbourhood of Kidderminster. To its north is Wolverley, whose Georgian church of 1772 is set up on a steep rock and reached by steps cut in the red sandstone. It is built of brick and battlemented and there are some charming classical memorials, one by Flaxman, as well as a fourteenth-century effigy of a knight which has survived from a former building. Sebright School, founded in 1620, is largely in the Gothic style; once it had a considerable name in Worcestershire educational circles as one of our minor public schools. Then, recently, and quite suddenly, it ceased to be a public school at all and became yet another casualty of the inflationary situation. There are cave dwellings and a circular ice house cut into the solid rock near here and a few fine Georgian houses.

Cookley, again to the north, has a rather dull church of 1849 and 1872 and Broome, to the east, is a very small eighteenth-century church in a delightful rural setting, with a Norman font and an east end added in 1861. Further east is Belbroughton, a church of Norman origins but containing much late Perpendicular work and some Jacobean carpentry. There is a fine Georgian rectory here, overlarge, whose fate as a parsonage house is still very much in the balance. Several other good dwelling houses of the same period may be noted in the village and around it. Finally in the country and this time south of Kidderminster we have Stone, with its typically 1831 church and an east window by Kempe.

Returning now to the main road, this north-eastern spoke passes through the villages of Churchill with a W. J. Hopkins church of

1868, and Blakedown where there are some remaining traces of a church built by G. E. Street in 1866. His fame as a Victorian architect was not sufficient to preserve the church which he designed against the addition of an aisle in 1905. To the east of the main road here is the timber-framed Harborough Hall, formerly the home of Major W. J. Thompson, to whom we owe the initiative for the preservation of Greyfriars in Worcester. It was bought by him after being scheduled for demolition in 1930 and handed over to the County Archaeological Society after he had carried out first-aid repairs. A useful room for meetings and the accommodation for the Society's library, adjoining the dwelling house at Greyfriars, now commemorates his generosity in its name, Thompson's Trust.

So we arrive at Hagley and the kingdom of the Lord Lieutenant, Lord Cobham. We had promised a pastoral interlude along this section of our spoke but, apart from Hagley Park and the Clent Hills which rise to the south-east of it, we are very much in Birmingham suburbia. At West Hagley, which we reach first, we are met by the typically suburban St. Saviour's Church of the beginning of the century, now thickly surrounded by elegant modern villas. But further on, with the main road forging ahead to the north-east in the direction of Halesowen we reach the real Hagley with its great park and house to the east.

There was a time when Hagley Hall stood pretty high in the stately homes stakes and was much visited by the public. But in recent years it has retreated again into domestic privacy somewhat to the consternation of the culture-mongers but to the greater ease of its inmates. The culture-mongers are a little to be pitied for if Worcestershire has a show place this is indeed it, ranking with Croome Court which in its institutional use is also more or less inaccessible to the public. Here is Palladio again, mediated by Inigo Jones as at Wilton, executed by Sanderson Miller. The affinities with Croome are obvious and both share with Wilton those corner pyramidal turrets so characteristic of the style. The house has been singularly fortunate. It was seriously damaged by fire in 1925 and most carefully restored in 1926 so that the stucco of Vassali can still be appreciated by connoisseurs. The theme is rococo and those who delight in that style will find, particularly in the Dining Room, a wide variety of subjects ingeniously delineated. The Gallery is a room of impressive proportions and both here and elsewhere in the house are choice examples of the furniture of the period.

The name of Sanderson Miller might have suggested as at Lacock, an exercise in the Strawberry Hill Gothick for Hagley, but whilst adhering in the house to strict Palladian models the architect appears to have let his fancy free in the rebuilding of the nearby parish church. Unfortunately his work was superseded by a later hand. There is a little medieval work surviving and Rickman built a north arcade and aisle in 1826. Then came Street, who between 1858 and 1865 so added to it that what we principally see now is a Victorian church with a broach spire.

But there are other delights at Hagley besides the house and church. The garden ornaments include the Temple of Theseus by 'Athenian Stuart', which is the earliest example of the revival of Grecian architecture to be found anywhere. It dates from 1758 and is a miniature copy of its original in Athens. An Obelisk on the north side of the main road appears to be in pretty bad shape at present. There is also the Prince of Wales's Column near the church and the Castle, which is as pretty a piece of Sanderson Miller's Gothick experimentation as could be imagined. It dates from 1747 and Horace Walpole knew all about it, and approved. It reminded him of 'the true rust of the Barons' Wars'.

It is a pity that nothing of the Leasowes survives, for this was a celebrated venue for eighteenth-century travellers and very much part of the classical complex of the neighbouring Hagley. William Shenstone lived here from 1745 and devoted his time to the creation of a garden which attained much fame among the cognoscenti of the age. Everybody had to go and see it for no English tour was complete without it. Dr. Johnson praised it highly and John Wesley thought that nothing in Europe could touch it. Horace Walpole also applauded, rather with his tongue in his cheek. It inspired Shenstone, its creator, to write romantic verses. Now it is all gone except for a fragment of the 'ruinated priory', and a golf course covers the former pleasure grounds. We should be grateful that so much of Hagley itself has been preserved for us and that it is carefully watched and tended by its present owner, who represents a family whose impact on the County has been so influential. The rights and wrongs of the Dissolution of the Monasteries will be long debated; schoolboys, no doubt, will be required to discuss in examination papers whether they were an economic anachronism in the developing new nationhood of the sixteenth century. A schoolboy who attempted to justify Henry VIII might do worse than adduce the emergence of such families as the Lytteltons, who were enriched by the spoils of Halesowen Abbey, as putting a good deal back in recompense for their enhanced wealth by the continuing service which such families have paid to Church and State.

It must be one of the few disadvantages of being an aristocrat that the fierce light which plays around the throne occasionally overspills to illuminate some of the murkier upper branches of the family tree. We ordinary mortals whose recorded forebears fade out somewhere about 1850 have not to suffer the scrutiny of busy-bodying historians who are apt to denominate those pioneers of noble families under the categories of good and bad. It is a pity from the point of view of the moralist that the good are so often dull and the bad infinitely more exciting. Two such Lytteltons apparently adorned the eighteenth century. The first, a statesman and also a minor poet and a scholar who wrote a long book on Henry II and was vigorously criticised by such eminent *littérateurs* of the age as Gibbon, Smollett, Dr. Johnson and Cobbett, nevertheless has been handed down to posterity as 'good'. His son, the second Lord Lyttelton, over whose precise wickedness a veil must be decently drawn has been firmly placed in the opposite category. He has a certain fame in Spiritist circles by reason of a remarkable dream prophesying his death. The first 'good' lord does not seem to have made a very good Chancellor of the Exchequer. Joseph Farington, the artist diarist has a delightful note about him at the turn of the century. He was a statesman who, the diarist says, was 'a very absent man, of formal manners, who never laughed'. He was apt to be an embarrassment to mixed company as when he embarked on a description of 'the generation of Bees with many particulars, which put the ladies into some confusion'. As Chancellor of the Exchequer, Farington says he 'was unqualified for the office, being so defficient in knowledge of figures that he often made a jumble in his reports to the House, mistaking half-pence for guineas. He was formal and singular in his dress. Lord Oxford once called on him when he was recovering from an illness and found him dressed in a Brocade coat, with a night cap on.'

However, in the respectable Victorian century, the Lytteltons, like the Monarchy and other aristocratic families who took their cue from it, seem to have shared the prevailing taste for scholarship combined with rectitude. A Victorian Lord Lyttelton was a Greek scholar who made translations of English poems and his family sustained a reputation for statesmanship and cricket which is still with us. Could it really have been true that the cricketing sons practised their strokes and bowling in the long gallery at Hagley?

William Gladstone was a favourite visitor to the Hall, his wife and the wife of the reigning Lord Lyttelton being sisters. An old man of our acquaintance, whose early life had been much connected with horses, once told us, with much pride, how, in his youth he had driven 'Billy Gladstone' round Hagley Park. The present gracious representative of the family, Lord Cobham, amply sustains the family traditions of statesmanship and scholarship. As senior official in the Royal Household and as Governor General of New Zealand he has given great service to his country, and his printed speeches delivered in New Zealand are a model of the penetrating and lucid use of the English language. As Lord Lieutenant of the County he has endeared himself to Worcestershire people by the invariable courtesy and friendliness of his manner.

No doubt it was because of his Hagley visits that Mr. Gladstone seems to have had a special fondness for Romsley church, to which he was a generous donor. This little church on the east side of the Clent Hills is dedicated in honour of St. Kenelm who is supposed to have been a boy king of Mercia, murdered here in 819. Both propositions are open to doubt, but *pace* local legend, there truly is a holy spring at the east end of the church which in the arbitrary manner of such springs is reputed to have burst forth at the spot where he was killed. However, St. Kenelm's church is certainly a building of much antiquity, probably of the pre-Conquest foundation. Its fifteenth-century tower seems disproportionately thin, but there is twelfth- and fourteenth-century work inside and a fine twelfth-century tympanum. The monks of Halesowen Abbey seem to have made a good thing, in days when such habits were prevalent, of offerings at the spring shrine of St. Kenelm.

With our Clent and Lickey Hills in our north-east corner we do indeed arrive at the pastoral delights foreshadowed, delights much appreciated by the thousands of Birmingham excursionists who flock southwards for their picnics on the hills. The Clent Hills lie east of Hagley Park, between there and Romsley. They extend for five miles and can be ascended by paths from Clent Village or from the outskirts of Halesowen. There are romantic bits of country to be explored here, and there are elevated points—the highest being Walton Hill, about 1,000 ft., from which extensive views can be obtained. The Wrekin on one side and the Malvern range on the other provide fine vistas. And there are archaeological sites to be noted; Wychbury Hill was a British camp and five British burial barrows are near by. The discovery of Roman coins near Wychbury indicates continuous occupation of this area from earliest times. The village of Clent, with its church largely rebuilt in 1865, lies in a fold of the hills; the chancel and tower, late fifteenth-century work, remain from the former church. The Amphletts, a well-known Worcestershire name, were the principal family here and there are memorials to them in the church. The interior is unusual in sloping up from west to east.

Part of the Lickey Hills is also within the County, with their highest point Beacon Hill rising to 987 ft. The Lickey Church of 1856 is unexceptional and Wythall, by Preedy in the Butterfield style of 1862 is redeemed by a magnificent tower of 1903 by W. H. Bidlake. We are on the County boundary here, very close to suburban Solihull and only seven or eight miles from the centre of Birmingham.

Now we must proceed along the boundary which runs north to Halesowen and here we certainly encounter one of our few Worcestershire industrial towns. But if all this neighbourhood gives the impression of a complex of chemical works and steel works and chain and fire-brick making, it is to be remembered that Halesowen was an important ecclesiastical centre long before the blessings of iron and steel manufacture dawned upon it. Yet there was warning of things to come when coal was mined in the vicinity as early as 1274. The medieval importance of the town rested in its great parish church and its abbey. A good deal remains of the former; very little of the latter. The church occupies a prominent site in the middle of the town. A good proportion of its Norman original survives, including a splendid font, all dating from 1150 to 1160, and most of the later work including the tower and spire come from the Perpendicular period. There are some good Norman details and mouldings, but much of the Norman character of the building was obscured in the fifteenth century when the tower and east part of the nave collapsed and the church had then to be more or less rebuilt in the contemporary style.

Little of the Abbey remains and what there is is a good deal involved in later farm buildings. It is situated about a mile south-east of the church and was a Premonstratensian foundation of 1214 resulting from a grant of the manor of Hales by King John to Peter, Bishop of Winchester. The remains date from between 1220 and 1230; the most extensive piece is practically the whole of the south wall of the nave and some bits of the chancel and the south transept. Of the conventual buildings there is the south wall of the refectory with windows and buttresses, and there are also remains of a building which may have been the abbot's house or the guest house. There survive only two monuments, a fourteenth-century knight with crossed legs and a thirteenth-century coffin lid. Some excavation has been attempted in recent years and no doubt when further opportunity offers there is a good deal more of interest to be revealed.

This is not a predominantly Georgian town, though a few eighteenth-century buildings remain and Halesowen has not escaped its inevitable quota of modern high-risers. One Victorian villa, still a doctor's house, has a certain personal interest. It was the home of Francis Brett Young, himself a doctor's son, from whence he commuted to Birmingham University when he was a medical student. Besides the intense regional interest of his Worcestershire novels, with their vivid evocation of the Worcester countryside in the Wyre Forest and elsewhere and their portrayal of this town under the pseudonym of 'Halesby', the novels betray the close acquaintance with medical practice which might be expected from one who had studied medicine.

We have already referred to the scarcity of Worcestershire regional novelists and there might be opportunity here to mention, though with no immediate reference to this locality, Brett Young's greatest predecessor. That was Mrs. Henry Wood whose name is commemorated on a tablet over a house in Sidbury, where she grew up, which reminds us of 'Danesbury House'. In her novels 'Helstonleigh' is Worcester and the 'Channings' has some of its action around the Cathedral which also has another memorial to her. No less a weighty authority than Mr. Justice Avory, when unveiling this tablet in 1916, recounted that 5,750,000 copies of her *East Lynne* had by that time been sold. The dramatised version of that famous tear-jerker was probably the most famous play ever produced and could even draw an audience when Shakespeare failed. We ourselves remember it being presented, in a very freely adapted way, by a company of travelling players in a Somerset barn in 1934. As a best seller, our Worcester authoress must come a very good second to the Bible.

Of other churches in Halesowen there is little to be said. Hasbury, of brick and from 1907, is singularly conventional and unenterprising but Lapel, one of the few modern churches in the Worcester Diocese, has been quite adventurous in its experimenting with those zig-zag façades in which a very distinguished modern ecclesiastical building may have set a fashion. Indeed, to borrow an idea invented by the greatest of Smiths, Lapel church looks rather as though Coventry Cathedral had come down to Halesowen and pupped; the offspring is much to be applauded.

Another of our northern towns, Stourbridge, must be explored. We reach it by returning to Hagley so that we may approach it through its pleasant suburbs of Pedmore and Old Swinford. Pedmore has grown enormously in recent years, but there is still a green oasis around the church. Wychbury Hill towers above it and the fine Regency rectory still survives, though it was too big by modern clerical standards and was secularized a few years ago; but the church, the bulk of which is by Preedy in 1871, contains a surprise. There is a splendid Norman tympanum over the door which shows again the Herefordshire influence with a Christ figure in an almond-shaped glory, wearing a crown and with his hand raised in blessing. There are other curious animal and bird devices in the design and other Norman fragments survive in the church. Cricket is still played in a village atmosphere on a field adjoining the church and the modern public house provides an admirable setting for suburban drinkers. Thus Pedmore has nearly everything.

With Old Swinford you are almost in Stourbridge; but this is quite the most attractive part of the town and has much to offer. The church, of red sandstone, is a rebuilding from 1842 and is rather too wide for its length, though Chatwin's chancel of 1898 gives it an added dignity and the spire is tall and impressive, the only part of the medieval church remaining and dating from the late fourteenth century.

The 1700 rectory, with, happily, the parson still living there, is a delightful house in the Wren idiom; not so fine as Hartlebury, but one of the dozen or so notable parsonage houses in the County. The circumstances of its building by Dr. William Hallifax are fully revealed by papers which are preserved in the County Record Office. The rector was very anxious to have a new house, for his parsonage, he said, 'was a very old timber building and in great decay and though it stood upon 72 foot of ground in length . . . there were but 3 rooms in the whole range with 3 little ones of small considera-tion and but 2 chambers with chimneys and one without . . .'. After the usual irksome delays which attend all building projects, the rector eventually got his new dwelling, which is the one we see as happily in use to the present day.

The gates and walls of the churchyard, designed by Sir Giles G. Scott, were handsomely provided by the generosity of the late Mr. Ernest Stevens, a manufacturer of enamel ware, who in his pros-perity was not unmindful of his native town. Stourbridge is indebted to him for a Maternity Hospital and two parks as well as lesser benefactions. It is a pity that the town showed so little appreciation of his generosity that the handsome ironwork gates of one of the parks found its way to a scrap heap as a result of a recent municipal enthusiasm for unfenced spaces. In this Old Swinford enclave is also the Old Hall, a handsome mid-eighteenth-century house and the early nineteenth-century Castle which formerly was suitably castel-lated, but which has now lost its castellations in a recent ruthless piece of restoration. Some pretty cottages make all this a very charming backwater, but modern building invades and the Castle grounds have spawned a housing estate.

We have already encountered the Foleys at Great Witley, where they established themselves when their iron fortune was secure. But the Old Swinford Hospital is impressive evidence that they, like the modern enamel manufacturer, did not forget the needs of their native place. The original buildings, founded by Thomas Foley in 1670, fortunately survive, all three of them, built of brick in three stories and with gables, the middle block adorned with a turret and cupola. The doorway is an involved piece of Renaissance ingenuity. The whole pile sits with great dignity beyond an expanse of grass and provides an impressive introduction to the town to the left of the main road as you enter.

Stourbridge could hardly be called 'Black Country'. Although manufacture is so near, it still preserves the atmosphere of a market town and a gyratory road system does its best to deal with the bustle of modern traffic at the centre. Glass is the foundation of the town's prosperity which began with the coming of Huguenot refugees in the sixteenth century. The local clay was a valuable element at one stage of the manufacture which grew to great prosperity in the nineteenth century. Some of the finest modern glass is still made there and examples of its most exotic products are impressively displayed in show cases in the Council House which was formerly Studley Court; its gift to the town is another example of the generosity of Mr. Ernest Stevens.

Since Old Swinford had the ancient parish church of the neighbourhood, it is not surprising to find a Georgian church at the centre of the town, which must have been growing greatly in importance when it was built. And a very good specimen, too, is St. Thomas, which dates from 1728 with an apse added by Bidlake in 1890; it is one of the best of the County's classical churches. St. John's is not a particularly distinguished example of Street's work and the Roman Catholic church is by the younger Pugin. The High Street has a few good Georgian buildings and the most interesting in the town is probably the Talbot Inn, formerly a house of the Foley family, which dates from the seventeenth century and has some good contemporary interior plaster work, though it was refronted in the eighteenth century. Stourbridge has an ancient Grammar School, a re-endowed Edward VI foundation, but the present buildings date from 1862 onwards with fairly recent additions.

Wollaston, part of Stourbridge, deserves a mention because Wollaston Hall, a seventeenth-century timbered house, now demolished, was the original home of the Foley family to whom much of the industrial prosperity of the neighbourhood is due; its church, school and parsonage, in blue bricks, were by Bidlake in 1860, but the last was demolished and a new house built in a more usual hue about 1965. Amblecote, the northern part, has an important modern hospital and a wide early Victorian church by Perkins, made of yellow glazed brick, entirely congruous to such a neighbourhood, and yet with a surprisingly convincing facsimile of a Perpendicular tower which might have come from the Cotswolds.

One part of this northern industrial Worcestershire remains to be described and we have to go through Staffordshire to reach it, for it is that bit of the scorched pie crust which has become entirely separated from the main County, and makes a little island oı Worcestershire in a sea of Staffordshire. This is the town of Dudley. Our northern spoke has now broken its bounds and projects beyond the rim of our Worcestershire wheel; we follow it, leaving that fine tower of Amblecote on the right and traversing the Staffordshire Brierley Hill, so as to re-enter 'Worcestershire—detached' as the map says. Whatever may be the future arrangements of civic government we must still insist on Dudley belonging, spiritually at any rate, to Worcestershire, for it is part of its history and tradition. It is a county borough with over 50,000 inhabitants and its prosperity has rested upon its deposits of limestone and coal and iron. Besides, it contains the only genuine castle in the County; Worcester's castle disappeared long ago. But here is a splendid ruin, fit to vie with its better-known neighbour at Kenilworth in the next county. It was sufficiently important to be mentioned in the Domesday Book, though there is little that is Norman surviving now. There is twelfth-century work but the great gatehouse dates from about 1320. The keep also is of the period and the chapel and what was originally the great chamber were built in the middle of the fourteenth century. Sir John Dudley, later Duke of Northumberland, obtained the castle in 1533 and he initiated a building programme, much of which remains with the ruined great hall with its square-headed mullioned windows. There is much that has survived from every period, although

196

the official dismantling took place in 1647, and it is indeed a historic monument of the greatest importance.

Dudley Castle has been fortunate in its ultimate fate, for it now contains the animals and birds of a most impressive zoo and is probably one of the most popular picnic venues in the Midlands. It is a happy circumstance that such a use has been found for a redundant castle; it is a pity that it is not possible to use redundant churches and parsonages in the same way. Dudley Castle stands on a hill which dominates the town, proud above the smoke and the blast furnaces, and there is another hill, delightfully named Wren's Nest, which is now a conservation reserve.

If it is true that Dudley with misplaced civic pride has sometimes called itself 'the capital of the Black Country' it has done itself less than justice. For again, as at Stourbridge, it retains much of the atmosphere of a somewhat enlarged country town, with its High Street rising from 'bottom church' to 'top church' and busy, at times, with the bustle of a thriving street market. You may easily discover tree-lined squares and skilfully laid out public gardens tucked away behind the houses and shops; there is a second but sham castle and the tidied-up ruins of a Cluniac Priory founded in the middle of the twelfth century and afterwards a cell of Wenlock Abbey. So Dudley must not belittle itself unless it believes that it is grander to reign a Queen of blackness than to make the most of its resemblance to a Worcestershire country town with a 'County atmosphere'.

St. Edmund's Church, 'bottom church', a medieval foundation, which lay in ruins for 80 years and was then rebuilt in 1724 is a Georgian gem that would grace any London square. St. Thomas, 'top church', also medieval in origin but now retaining only an altar slab from its remote past, is a superb example of Regency Gothick, built in 1817. It has a splendid spire and the best that the age could do in the way of vaulting and statues in niches, a fantastic interlude between the Gothick of Strawberry Hill and the veridical achievements of Scott and Street. Its east window with its 1821 painted glass, though described by Mr. Matley Moore as 'unfortunately' remaining, would surely be more unfortunate in its removal. It is delicious in its interpretation of the Ascension; and its charm surely derives from what Mr. Matley Moore describes as Our Lord executing 'an elegant

197

pas seul to the admiration of two buxom winged ladies in the base who look like celestial barmaids'. Certainly we have travelled far from the glories of Italian mosaics and Botticelli angels, but how much less joyous would be the panoply of our native ecclesiology if we were to jettison all such absurdities. Anyhow, we are told that Dudley thinks a lot of its celestial barmaids. Long may they survive for its enjoyment!

This is the end of our northern spoke, but it has penetrated only into the eastern end of our northern frontier and justice demands that we skim briefly along the rest of the frontier, travelling west until we reach the end of the first spoke with which we began when we followed the Teme Valley as far as that spoke's end in Tenbury. It is a delightful range of country and our east-to-west route quickly brings us north and west of Kidderminster to another surviving bit of the once thickly wooded territories of Worcestershire in Wyre Forest, which bestrides the boundary with Shropshire. There are miles of remote forest land here which make the so-called Black Country so recently left behind, seem a thousand miles away. Brett Young has made this territory very much his own in some of his delightful Worcestershire novels, and there really is a Far Forest, though there is nothing particularly romantic in its church built by Preedy in 1844. But there are charming names like Eymore Wood and Button Oak and Pound Green and Hawkbatch to be explored; and who could resist the sylvan sound of Coachroad Coppice and Doghanging Coppice and Wimperhill Wood? And there are many other mellifluous names to indicate now lucky Wyre Forest was in having missed the industry which compelled the Forest of Feckenham to yield its timber to feed the furnaces of the salt-makers of Droitwich.

Yet one more glorious church remains to be described in this neighbourhood, just south of the forest, at Rock. High and lifted up, it is reputed to serve the largest ecclesiastical parish in England; whether this be true or not, its acreage amounts to 8600. It is a noble church, the largest Norman village church in the County. Perhaps its very remoteness preserved it from over-much restoration and the onslaughts of advancing architectural styles. The flat buttresses of nave and chancel proclaim the Norman origin and there are decorated corbels and shafted windows and capitals with scallops and

31 (opposite above) Glasshampton – Early nineteenth-century stables for twentieth-century Franciscans

32 (below) Bewdley – eighteenth century inland port

fluted leaves. Within, there are grotesque sculptures which take you back again to the Shobdon arches of the Herefordshire sculptors and the font, too, is Norman work. Of course, later periods are represented in the Decorated chancel window and the Perpendicular tower; and of course there had to be Victorian restoration or preservation and Preedy did it very well in 1861. Because the impression here is that little has been spoilt, Rock is the last triumphant flourish of that Norman spirit of which we have found so much surviving evidence and which has given us so much pleasure as we have journeyed through the County.

33 (*opposite above*) *Hagley – Palladian palace*
34 (*below*) *Ombersley – Rickman Church and fourteenth-century mausoleum*

Epilogue

Such is the shape of Worcestershire today and such are the sites and monuments which remain to mark the progress of that sweep of County history which was sketched in the introduction. But the wind of change has blown fiercely around us and already some of the new civil arrangements are facts accomplished. Worcestershire has lost its separate identity and has been merged in a new Hereford–Worcester County. The name for this new combination was keenly canvassed for a period. Elgarshire was perhaps rightly rejected as representing only one strand in the neighbourhood's cultural tradition. Wyevern had a little more relevance and was an ingenious evocation of two important water ways; Malvern County was suggested. But those ideas had to give way to the simpler and more straightforward Hereford–Worcester which at any rate does not sound any worse than the name of a respectable building society. All this is to come very shortly into operation and the new County Council of Hereford and Worcester has already been elected. Worcester City Council loses its autonomy in the new amalgamation and local administrative districts are reduced from 29 to 9. The Worcestershire which we have been investigating has been so enlarged that the rim of the new county will cover 230 miles, contain nearly a million acres and provide living space for half a million people.

It is not for mere historians even to comment, much less to pass judgment on this new structuring. The only way in which they can have any interest is the extent to which the new authority is interested in the problems of archaeological preservation. Local authorities now have much power in controlling the fortunes of historical buildings whose future is in doubt. Preservation orders are extremely powerful in restraining the activities of over-eager demolishers, and money for conservation projects is generously available for those who take the trouble to find out how to obtain it. It is by no means outside the bounds of possibility that the State may extend a generous hand to the maintenance of church fabrics which at the moment are largely dependent on voluntary support. If the Church can bring itself to shed the ecclesiastical exemption clause in the 1913 measure which opened the way for State grants for historic buildings, there is no telling what doors may be opened for financial help for churches and chapels which, after all, are among our principal historical monuments and which now, only too often, are steadily deteriorating for want of adequate means to provide for their repair and upkeep. Continental governments have a good deal to teach us in this field. Our only concern with present governmental reorganisation is as to whether every new local authority will exercise its powers of civil aid to the full with increasing pride in the survival of all that is worthwhile in our building heritage.

Much of the prosperity of Worcestershire in former times was based on the Severn. When Sabrina, the river goddess, had carried on her bosom the merchandise of the Indies which she deposited on the quays of Upton and Bewdley, the hinterland of the County became accessible to the trade of the world. The little Severn trows darted hither and thither on the surface of the water pursuing the daily business of ordinary diligent men. But all this languished with the coming of the Victorian century and the quays mouldered, neglected and unused. Then, in the second part of our century another great highway has been riven through the heart of our County, not a water road, but a broad road of stone and concrete whose lanes of traffic are already too few to sustain the loads of merchandise which an ever-increasing freight of motor cars and lorries and container vans must lay upon it.

M.5 enters our County at Strensham in the south and leaves it at Chadwich on the outskirts of Birmingham; it skirts Worcester and Droitwich and Bromsgrove on its route and as it leaves the County it bids farewell, on its left, to a fine Caroline manor house with hipped roof and flat quoins and characteristic late seventeenth-century windows. At Chadwich Manor all seems in good order, quite as it should be. But when it entered the County at Strensham the situation was rather different. Away on the right the traveller might have noted this name on his map and he would have been well rewarded had he had time to go and look at that church. Perhaps not an outstanding building, yet it contains some of the principal treasures among our church furnishings. There is a wonderful west gallery its front painted with the figures of 23 saints from the last decade of the fifteenth century. There are two of the best brasses in the County to members of the Russell family and there are tomb chests and alabaster effigies to other members of the family and a Stanton marble monument to Sir Francis Russell who died in 1705. And there are other treasures, tiles and silver too. But the traveller who paused and diverted from M.5 would have been shocked to have discovered that the home of this distinguished family is now nothing more than an empty ruin, like Witley Court; perhaps not so impressive a house, 1824, neo-classical with a great portico and unfluted Ionic columns. But the place has its literary traditions, for the church has a memorial to Samuel Butler whose father was a Worcestershire farmer and church-warden of the parish who wrote the details of his son's christening in the baptism register of the parish. Butler is said to have written his fiercely anti-Puritan poem *Hudibras* at the Ketch Inn at Kempsey.

There is something of an allegory here, something preserved and something in the final stages of decay. Perhaps we can well dispense with Strensham Court; it was not a particularly important house and there are more precious things in Worcestershire. But Strensham is representative; valuable things prized and protected, side by side with other things uncared for and lost. This is what we are seeing throughout the County and perhaps more particularly in the city itself. If, as we said at the beginning, a travel book has any value it is to be a record, as here in the '70s, of what Worcestershire people thought was worth preserving, what had recently disappeared, and what, like Strensham Court, was on the way out. Mistakes have been made which ought not to have been made; carelessness and apathy have lost forever things that ought not to have been lost. But take heart; *conservation* is a blessed word today and the Ministry of the Environment is on the side of the angels.

Redundancy, however, is a different word altogether. Several times we have had sadly to use it in connection especially with some of our ecclesiastical buildings, churches and fine old parsonages. Must we accept that situation and bid some of our churches farewell as relics of the inexorable forward march of an expanding capitalistic economy? Are they merely symbols of a superseded philosophy in a consumer society which has discarded its spiritual dimension and thinks little of the numinous value of hallowed places and long familiar uses? Or are there still sufficient people who care deeply about these things, who love to visit the sort of places that have been touched upon lightly and inadequately in this book and who make what contribution they can to their preservation? Such people, we believe, are those who, perhaps unwittingly, are trying to disentangle what seems to them timeless and abiding from what is merely brash and transient in our contemporary situation. Dare we speak of this as a spiritual exercise, for these abiding things are an avenue to an appreciation of that beauty which is one of the few manifestations we can grasp of the nature of the Creator Spirit. Antiquarian and artistic pursuits, we are persuaded, are never time squandered, for they lead ultimately to a deepening of the metaphysical dimension. Such an exercise is perhaps easier in Worcestershire than in many other places.

Index

Abberley, Church 77; Hall 77; The Elms 78; Rectory 78; spoons 77
Adam Brothers, architects 45, 112, 113
Alcock, Bishop John 100
Aldwin, Monk of Malvern 87, 100
Alexander, G. 185
Alfrick 70
Alvechurch 141
Amblecote 196
Ankerdine Hill 69, 87
Areley Kings 24, 152, 166, 168
Arley, Upper 176
Arthur, Prince of Wales 28, 176
Arts and Crafts Movement 155, 156
Art Nouveau 156
Ashton-under-Hill 125
Astley 16, 22, 39, 161, 162
Astwood Bank 139, 140
Atkins, Sir Ivor 84
Avon, River 19, 114, 129, 134
Avoncroft Museum 47, 61
Augustine, St. 20, 180

Badby of Evesham 26
Badsey 19, 133
Bagutti, P. M. 76
Baldwin, Earl, of Bewdley 45, 162, 171, 176; Alfred 165, 171, 174
Bannut Tree Farm, Castle Morton 85, 105
Barcheston 141
Barker, Philip 24
Barry, T. D. 130
Bartlett, Arthur 155
Baxter, Richard 31, 63, 132, 184, 185
Bayton 79
Beauchamp, Sir John 26; Sir Richard 27, 144; Lord 15; family 24, 84, 144, 160; tombs 184

Beckford 124, 125
Beguildy 82
Belbroughton 186
Bellamy, Thomas 101
Bellucci, Antonio 76
Bengeworth 129
Beoley 140
Berkeley, family 136; hospital 52
Berrow 105; Green 69
Berrow Hill 19, 87
Berrows Worcester Journal 36
Besford 118
Bewdley 19, 39, 162, 171, 174–176, 203
Bidlake, W. H. 191, 195, 196
Birlingham 118
Birmingham 139, 141, 191
Birt, Bradley 104
Birtsmorton 28, 39, 104
Black Death 26
Blackstone Rock 174
Blakedown 187
Blomfield, Sir Arthur 96, 103, 155, 174
Blore, Edward 106
Blount Tombs, at Astley 166; at Kidderminster 184
Blow, Detmar 143
Bodley, G. F. 142
Bonaparte, Lucien 159
Bordesley Abbey 29, 140, 141
Boulton, R. 159
Brakspear, Sir Harold 116
Brandon, David 102, 152, 154
Bray, Sir Reginald 27
Brecknell, John 183
Bredon 21, 81; church 119; Hill 19, 40, 69, 108, 121
Bredon's Norton 20, 121, 122; Manor 122, 123

Bretforton, 132
Brindley, James 170, 175
Britten family 65
Broadheath 65
Broadwas 64
Broadway 19, 108, 130, 131
Brock, Sir Thomas 41, 184, 186
Brockhampton, Herefs. 118, 155
Bromsgrove 19, 153, 154; Guild 156; School 154, 155
Bromyard 69
Brookhampton 180
Broome 186
Broughton Hackett 22, 137, 138
Brown, Lancelot ['Capability'] 80, 112, 113
Browning, Elizabeth B. 99
Buckingham, Duke of 27
Bullingham, Bishop Nicolas 30
Burne-Jones, Sir Edward 165, 172, 174
Burrough, Tom 97
Bushley 106
Butler, Samuel 34, 204
Butterfield, William 125, 139, 141, 142
Byfield, George 133, 143

Caerleon 19
Callow End 84
Cantelupe, Bishop Walter de 24, 57, 173
Cap industry, Bewdley 175
Caractacus 20, 80
Carpenter, Bishop John 88
Carpenter, Richard C. 124
Carpet Industry, Kidderminster 185
Cassian, St., Chaddesley Corbett 156
Castle Morton 105
Catesby, Robert 30
Chaddesley Corbett 22, 155, 156
Chadwich Manor 203
Chandos, Duke of 76
Chantrey, Sir Francis 45, 142, 152
Charles I, King 32, 33, 36, 139
Charles II, King 34, 36; house 51
Charles, F. W. B. 47, 68
Charles-Edwards, Mrs. 173
Charlton 19
Château Impney, Droitwich 15, 148
Cheriton Abbot 126
Chipping Campden 53, 130, 176
Churchill, nr. Kidderminster 186
Churchill, nr. White Ladies Aston 137, 138

Churchill, Sir Winston 165
Cider fruit 70, 80
Civil War 32–34, 47, 63, 102, 173
Claines 143
Clayton and Bell, Glass 45, 86, 101
Cleeve Prior 133
Clent 191; hills 19, 178, 187, 190, 191
Clifton-on-Teme 66, 71
Coade Stone 143
Cobbett, William 40, 189
Cobham, the Rt. Hon. Lord 15, 187, 190
Cockerell, Sir Sydney 84
Cogswell, W. G. St. John 140
Cole, J. J. 77
Collins Green 69
Colvin, H. M. 52
Combertons, The 124
Comhampton 180
Comper, Sir N. 97
Coningsby Wall, Areley Kings 169
Cookes family 142, 161; Sir Thomas 154
Cookley 186
Cookesey memorials, St. Mary, Kidderminster 184
Copley, Thomas 122, 123, 142
Corbett, John 147
Cotheridge 64
Cotswold Hills 69, 108, 130
Cotton, John 155
Coughton Court 134
Coventry family 111
Cowleigh [Malvern] 97
Crabbs Cross 140
Cranston, James 71
Craycombe House, Fladbury 133, 143
Cromwell, Oliver 32
Croome D'Abitot 15, 113; Court 39, 111, 112, 143, 187
Cropthorne 21, 133, 134
Crossway Green 180
Crowle 137

Davidson, Archbishop Randall 166
Dawkes, Samuel 72, 76, 77
Day, Charles 54, 140
Deanesly, Miss Margaret 155
Dee, Dr. John 103
Deykes, John and Samuel 94
Dissolution of the Monasteries 29, 189; Bordesley 140; Evesham 126; Halesowen 192; Little Malvern 100; Malvern 88; Pershore 115; Westwood 150; Worcester 28, 29

Doddenham 69
Dodderhill 148
Dodford 40, 155, 156
Domesday Book 22
Dormston 138
Doverdale 22, 180; Lord 150
Dowles Manor 158, 176
Drakes Broughton 111
Droitwich 19, 20, 24, 39, 144, 147, 178; St. Andrew's Church 148; St. Peter's Church 32, 148
Dudley 16, 178, 196; Castle 23, 25, 196, 197; St. Edmund's Church 197; St. Thomas's Church 197; family 41
Dunhampton 180
Dunstan, Saint 21

Earl's Croome 112
Eastham 79
Eckington 118
Edward, King IV 26, 175; VII 75; VIII 165; The Confessor 22
Eginton, H. 129, 131
Egwin, St. 126
Eldersfield 31, 105
Elgar, Sir Edward 15, 65, 99
Elizabeth, Queen, I. 30, 143, 150
Elmbridge 151
Elmley Castle 121, 123
Elmslie, E. W. 96
Esdaile, Mrs. K. A. 124, 130, 141
Evesham 19, 125–129; Abbey 21, 126; All Saints Church 126; Battle of 25; Almonry 126; Booth Hall 129; Campanile 126; St. Lawrence Church 129
Evesham, Epiphanius 119, 131

Far Forest 198
Farington, Joseph 189
Fawkes, Guy 30
Fawley, Bucks. 76
Feckenham 22, 139
Felindre 82
Fernhill Heath 143
Ferrey, Benjamin 118
Fielding, Henry 104
Fiennes, Celia 13
Finstall 155
Fladbury 21, 133, 134
Flaxman, John 186
Fleetwood, Bishop James 173
Florence, Chronicler 23

Flyford Flavell 137, 138
Fockbury 154
Foley, Richard 39, 72; Thomas 72 195; Lord 76
Forsyth, James 72, 76, 96
Fownes, Glovers 61
Fox, George 32
Franciscans, Anglican 162
Francisco 76
Friars 24
Froxmere Court 137

Galton family 149
Garnett, Father 31
Gauden, Bishop John 34
George III, King 36, 40
Gibbons, Grinling 71
Gibbs, James 52, 53, 76
Giffard, Bishop Godfrey 26, 59, 173; hotel 48
Giglis, Bishop John de 28
Gill, Eric 103
Gladstone, W. E. 190
Glass; Gt. Malvern 90; Stourbridge 195; Wilden 172
Glasshampton Monastery 161
Glendower, Owen 26, 78
Goodwin, Francis 184
Godwald, St. [or Gudwal] 155
Grafton Flyford 137, 138; Manor 154
Great Witley 16, 39, 72–77, 178
Greyfriars 24
Grimley 159
Guarlford 101
Gully, Dr. James 94, 95
Gunpowder Plot 30

Habershon, Matthew 153
Habington, Thomas 14, 30, 90, 142
Haddon Bros., Malvern 96
Hadzor 142, 149, 153
Hagley 15, 31, 39, 187–190, 193; West 187
Halesowen 22, 178, 191; abbey 189, 190, 192; church 191
Hall, Thomas 32
Hallifax, Dr. W. 194
Hallow 159
Ham, bridge 66, 71; castle 71
Hamilton, Duke of 34, 49
Hampstead, St. Johns 76
Hampton, Lord 150
Hamptons, The 180
Hampton Lovett 150, 151

Hanbury, 31, 151, 152
Hancock family 120, 122; school 120
Handel, G. F. 76, 81
Hanford, Monument, Eckington 119, 131
Hanley Castle 101; Child 80; Swan 101; William 80
Hansom, C. F. 96, 101
Harborough Hall 187
Hardman, John 45, 60, 101, 124
Hardwick, P. C. 85
Harmon Memorial, Kyre Wyard 80
Hartlebury 20, 172, 180; Castle 26, 39, 172, 173, 174; Church 172; Rectory 172; School 162, 172
Harvington Hall 30, 34, 157
Hasbury 193
Hastings family 68, 167; Sir Charles 68, 95
Heath, Bishop Nicholas 29
Henry VIII, King 28, 189
Hensley Henson, Bishop 166
Henwick 19
Hewell Grange 15, 31, 142
Hickes, Dean 35, 151
Hickes, Richard 141
Hill, Sir Rowland 186
Hindlip Hall 30, 31, 144
Hinton-on-the-Green 125
Hiorn, Francis 142
Hipplecote 69
Hodgetts, Mr. Michael 30, 144
Holbeach Hall 31
Holland-Martin family 122
Hollins, Humphrey 52
Holly Bush 87
Holt 159; Castle 26, 160; Church 16, 160; Fleet [bridge] 178
Hooper, Bishop John 29
Hop growing 69, 70
Hope End, Colwall 99
Hopkins, W. J. 61, 70, 111, 138, 140, 159, 171, 186
Horn Industry, Bewdley 175
Hough, Bishop John 35, 53
Housman, A. E. 121, 154
Huband family 141
Hugall, J. W. 101
Huddington 30, 31
Hundred Years War 26
Hunt, F. W. 97
Hurd, Bishop Richard 36; Library 173, 174
Huskisson, William 39, 104

Hussey, R. C. 149
Hwicce, The 20

Impney, Château 15, 148
Industrial Revolution 40, 42
Inkberrow 138, 139
Ipsley 141

Jackson, Sir Barry 98
John, King 23, 45, 101, 192
Johnson, Samuel 188, 189
Jones, Inigo 112, 187
Jones, Maurice 61, 97, 120, 134
Jones, John Joseph 77
Jones, Joseph 77

Katherine of Aragon 28, 176
Keck, Anthony 53, 103
Kemerton 121, 124
Kempe; Glass 70, 101, 140, 177, 186
Kempsey 19, 21, 25, 34, 106
Kenelm St. Romsley 190, 191
Kenswick, Manor 65
Kent, William 112
Kidderminster 19, 40, 178, 183–186, 198; churches 184, 185; industry 185
Kilvert, Francis 46, 58
Kingswood, Martley 65
Kington 138
Kipling, Rudyard 166
Knighton-on-Teme 79
Knightsford Bridge 69, 71
Knightwick 64, 69
Kyrewood House or Kyre Park 79
Kyre Wyard 79

Laguerre, Louis 76
Langland, William 26, 98
Lapel, Halesowen 193
Lasletts Almshouses 49, 125
Latimer, Bishop Hugh 28, 29
Laud, Archbishop William 31
Laugherne Brook 65; house 66
Lawson, Mrs. E. M. 102
Layamon of Areley Kings 24, 167, 168
Leasowes, Halesowen 39, 188
Lechmere family 15, 101
Lees-Milne, James 130
Leigh Sinton 70
Leintwardine 82
Leland, William 140, 153, 176
Lenches, The 132
Lenchford Hotel 160
Lewknor, Nicholas 142

Lichfield, Abbot 126, 129
Lickey Hills 16, 19, 178, 191; End 31
Lind, Jenny 98
Lindridge 19, 79
Little Malvern Priory 100; Court 100
Littleton, Sir Thomas 28
Littletons, The 132
Llewelyn the Great 25
Lloyd, Bishop William 35, 36
Longdon 105
Lords Marcher 25, 26
Ludlow 26, 28, 82, 176
Lulsley 70
Lygon family 84; Arms, Broadway 131
Lyttelton, Lords 29, 176, 189, 190

Macdonald, Alex 9; family 165
Maddox, Bishop Isaac 173
Madresfield 15, 44, 85
Malvern 87–99; Colleges 96; Great 29, 86; Link 86, 97; Wells 85, 99; West 97; Hills 15, 16, 19, 22, 44, 59, 69, 72; Priory 15, 87
Mamble 79
Martin family 122, 123; Mrs. V. Woodhull 122, 123
Martin Hussingtree 29, 143
Martley 65–69, 152, 167; Church 23, 67, 68; Rectory 67, 68; Schools 29; Union 67
Mere Hall 152
Midsummer Hill 19
Miller, Sanderson 112, 113, 187, 188
Misericord stalls; Gt. Malvern 90; Ripple 105
Mitton Chapel 167, 170
Montfort, Simon de 23, 24, 25, 126
Moor 133, 135
Moore, John 121; Matley 50, 197; Elsie 50; Temple 140
Morley, Bishop George 34
Morris, Thomas 35; William 172, 174
Mortimer, family, of Wigmore 175; Sir Hugh 27, 68
Mounteagle, Lord 31
Mountnorris, Lord 176, 177

Nail-making, Redditch 153
Nanfan family of Birtsmorton 28, 104
Nash, family of the Noak 50, 66, 67, 148; Dr. Treadway, County historian 14, 144
Naunton Beauchamp 137, 138

Needle-making, Redditch 140, 153
Nesfield, W. H. 72
Newland 85
Newtown 82
Nollekens, Joseph 45
Northampton 180
Norton-by-Kempsey 111; barracks 111
Norton-with-Lenchwick 131
Norton Park, Bredon's Norton 122

O'Connor, Feargus 40, 156
Oddingley 149
Offenham 133
Old Swinford 193, 194; hospital 195
Oldcorne, Fr. Ed. 31
Ombersley 15, 172, 178; Court 179
Ostorius 19, 20
Oswald, Saint 21, 22, 24
Ousley, Sir Frederick Gore 81
Overbury 122

Pakington family 66, 150, 157
Pancheri, R. 155, 156
Parker, J. F., Bewdley 173, 176
Parry, Gambier 86
Pedmore 193
Pendock 105
Peopleton 135, 137
Pepys, Bishop Henry 41
Perkins, A. E. 41, 69, 111, 196
Perrycroft, Colwall 85
Pershore 15, 21, 25, 29, 39, 114–118; Abbey 115, 116; St. Andrew 116
Pevsner, Sir Nikolaus 52, 58, 59, 70, 96, 105, 113, 116, 130, 134, 141, 174, 176
Philpott, Bishop Henry 41
Pinvin 133, 135
Pirton, Church 114, 138; Court 114; Rectory 114; Stone 114
Plowman, Piers 26, 98
Plymouth, Earls of 142
Pope, Alexander 36, 76; John 89
Porter's Mill, Claines 143
Powell, Glass 45, 101
Powick 44, 83; Bridge 32, 63, 82, 83; hospital 84
Poynter, Sir Edward 165
Prattinton, P. 14, 144, 175
Preedy, F. 51, 60, 85, 132, 133, 137, 140, 168, 191, 193, 198, 201
Price, J. 76
Prideaux, Bishop John 32, 33, 120
Prynne, W. H. Fellowes 60

Pudford Farm 51, 66
Pugin, A. W. N. 101, 137; E. W. 84, 195

Queenhill 105

Raban of Hadzor 149
Raleigh, Sir Walter 123
Redditch 139, 140, 153
Redmarley D'Abitot 40
Reed, Monument, Bredon 120
Reformation 26, 28, 29
Restoration, 1660 34
Revolution 35
Reynolds, G. Bainbridge 97
Rhydd Court 102
Ribbesford 174, 176
Rickman, Thomas 140, 172, 180, 188
Ricci, Sebastian 76
Ripple 21, 104
Rochford 79
Rock 16, 20, 198
Romsley 190
Ronkswood 61
Rose, James 78
Roses, Wars of 27
Roubilliac, L. F. 45, 152
Rous Lench 21, 32, 132
Rudhall, William 152
Rushock 35, 157
Russell, Henry 100
Russell, Hodgson and Leigh 48
Rysbrack, J. Michael 76

Salwarpe 144; Court 27
Sandon, Henry 48
Sandys, Bishop Edwin 30, 172; Lord 15, 179; memorials 130, 180
Savage family 124; Sir John 27
Scheemakers, Thomas 83
Scott, Sir George Gilbert 41, 45, 90, 97, 101, 106, 116, 170, 183; Sir Giles Gilbert 154, 184, 194
Sedding, J. D. 125
Sedgeberrow 125
Severn End 15, 101
Severn, River 39, 166, 170, 175, 203
Severn Stoke 106
Shaw, George Bernard 15, 84, 98
Shaw, Norman 85, 122
Sheldon family 140, 141
Shelsley Beauchamp 71
Shelsley Walsh 71, 72, 78
Shenstone, William 39, 188

Sheward, P. H. 103
Shrawley 152, 161
Shrewsbury 177
Simpson, Mrs., Duchess of Windsor 165
Sirr, Fr. William 161, 162
Smith, Brian 87
Smith, Sir Herbert 72, 185
Somers family 35
Spetchley 15, 33, 40, 135, 136
Spring Grove, Wribbenhall 174
Stafford family 27, 28, 153
Stanbrook Abbey 84
Stanford-on-Teme 40, 78
Stanmore, Lt. 76
Stanton family 45, 204
Stephen, King 23
Stevens, Ernest 194, 185
Stillingfleet, Bishop Edward 172; James 172
Stockton-on-Teme 78
Stoke Bliss 79
Stoke Prior 155
Stone 186
Stone, Nicholas 124
Storr, Archdeacon Vernon 166
Stoulton 111
Stour, River 39, 170
Stourbridge 31, 39, 178, 193, 195
Stourport-on-Severn 16, 39, 170, 171, 183
'Strawberry Hill Gothick' 53, 78, 113, 132, 173, 188, 197
Street, George Edmund 97, 149, 152, 187, 188, 195; family 50; A. E. 60
Strensham 203, 204
Studdert-Kennedy, Rev. G. A. 60
Suckley 70, 87
Summerfield 183
Sumner, Mary [née Heywood] 99
Sutton, Dr. Henry 120
Sytchampton 180

Talbot, Sir Gilbert 28, 153; Sir John 153
Talman, William 152
Tapper, Sir Walter 97
Tardebigge 142
Tasker, John 136
Telford, Thomas 176, 178
Teme, River 19, 27, 63–82, 178
Temple, Archbishop William 166
Tenbury Wells 21, 80, 81, 178, 198; St. Michael's College 81

Thomas, Bishop William 35
Thompson, W. J. 50, 187
Thorngrove, Hallow 137, 159
Thornhill, James 151
Three Choirs Festival 36
Three Counties Show 15
Throckmorton 133, 134
Tickenhill Palace 28, 173, 175, 176
Tiles, Malvern 64, 68, 90; Redditch 140
Tomkins, Thomas 29, 144
Townsend, Henry 32
Trent, River 39, 170
Tronquois, architect 148

Uphampton 180
Upper Arley 176
Upton Snodsbury 20, 137, 138
Upton Warren 151
Upton-on-Severn 33, 39, 53, 102, 104, 175, 203

Valentia, Lord 176
Vassali, F. 187
Vernon family 68, 151, 152, 167
Victoria, Queen 54, 80, 94
Voysey, C. F. A. 85, 105

Wailes, Glass 45
Wall, Dr. John 14, 48, 93
Wall, Fr. John 34, 157
Wall paintings: Dowles Manor 158; Harvington Hall 157; Martley 68
Walpole, Horace 141, 188
Ward, Lord 72
Waresley 183
Warmstry family 61
Watkins, W. 60
Webb, Sir Aston 16, 57, 70, 96, 143
Webb, J. 179
Welland 101
Wells, Randall 118
Wesley, John 36, 54, 188
Westmancote 121
Westwood, Droitwich 66, 149, 150, 178
Whall, Glass 45
Whiffen, Marcus 113
White, Thomas 52, 59
Whittington 111; Tump 19
White Ladies Aston 135, 137
White-Thomson, Bishop L. J. 166
Wichenford 65
Wickhamford 130
Wilkinson, Nathaniel 61

Wilden 171
Willis-Bund 32, 63
Willoughby, John 103
Wilson, Dr. James 94, 95
Wilson, Canon J. M. 84
Wilton, nr. Salisbury 187
Windsor family of Hewell 29
Winnington, Francis 35; Thomas 40
Winslow, Edward 32, 148
Wollaston 196
Wolsey, Cardinal 28, 104
Wolverley 186
Wood, Mrs. Henry 40, 193
Woodbury Hill 19, 27, 87
Woodhull-Martin, Mrs. V. 122
Woodmanton 71
Woodnorton 133
Woodward, Thomas 53, 176
Woodyer, Henry 81, 140
Woollas Hall 123
WORCESTER 43–62
    Alice Ottley School 53
    Barbourne 136, 143, 178
    Battles of 32, 33, 34, 49
    Berrow's Journal 36
    Blackfriars 24
    Britannia House 52, 53; Square 57
    Cathedral 15, 26, 43, 44 et seq., 176
    Churches
        All Saints 52, 58
        St. Andrew 61
        St. Barnabas 60
        St. Clement 60
        Countess of Huntingdon 59
        St. George 16, 57
        St. Helen 51
        Holy Trinity 47, 61
        St. John-in-Bedwardine 64
        St. Martin, Cornmarket 53
        St. Martin, London Rd. 60
        St. Matthew, Ronkswood 61
        St. Nicholas 25
        St. Paul 60
        St. Peter 60
        St. Stephen 60
        St. Swithun 53
    Commandery, 29, 34, 49, 155
    Deanery 46
    Deansway 44, 58, 59
    Dent, J. and W., gloves 61
    Edgar Tower 46
    Grammar schools 53, 57, 111, 137
    Greyfriars 24, 49, 187
    Guesten Hall, 47, 61

WORCESTER—*continued*
    Guildhall 16, 33, 36, 51, 52
    Industrial firms 61
    Infirmary 53
    Kay's Buildings 58
    King's School 46, 47, 53
    Old Palace 41, 46, 58
    Perdiswell Hall 143
    Porcelain works 14, 48
    Record office 51
    Regiment 111
    Sauce 14, 61
    Shire Hall 16, 54
    Sidbury 34, 49
    Star Hotel 58
    Swan theatre 58
    Technical college 16, 59, 61

Wren, Sir Christopher 52, 152, 172, 194
Wribbenhall 174
Wulfstan, Saint 22, 23, 24, 87, 155
Wychbold 151
Wylde, George 148
Wyntour family of Huddington 30
Wyre Forest 16, 192, 198
Wyre Piddle 21, 135
Wysham, Ralph 71

Yarranton, Andrew 39
York, Richard, Duke of 175
Young, Arthur 13
Young, Francis Brett 45, 133, 192, 198

Zattoni, Abbot 129